Introduction

Smartphones are brilliant inventions. They can help you send messages, video-call friends and family who are a long way away, and give you a feeling of closeness to those people who are precious to you. They enable you to listen to podcasts and music, as well as letting you take photos and videos that preserve precious memories. You can also play games, learn about pretty much anything and share your knowledge with other people. They are the best small computers you'll ever use. That's why most adults have one, and why children look up at their loving grown-ups and think, 'I want one of those too.'

Smartphones open a portal to the internet, this global computer network that's as vast as the sea. When you're playing in the sea it can be fun, but if you're not careful things can get tricky fast and unexpectedly. The sea often looks shallow by the shoreline, but you might sink waist-deep after a couple of steps. The water could well look clear, but there might be sharp rocks, slimy algae or spikey fish lurking under the sand. When frolicking in the sea, you might end up deeper than you meant to go or get pulled out by the current and end up far from safety.

Smartphones can feel a little like this too. They're incredibly useful tools, but they come with responsibilities and risks. There can be lots of things going on that you're not aware of at first glance. It's easy to click or swipe your way through the internet, but it can occasionally be tricky to find a way out. Sometimes too many clicks or swipes can mean you see things you didn't want to see or shouldn't be viewing at all, things that are scary, risky or harmful. The algorithms that are used on the internet might also mean this content is presented to you again and again. You might end up spending more time on your smartphone than you wanted to or even realise. This can mean that you're not devoting enough time to doing things you need to do offline, whether it be in relationships with others, getting out in the fresh air, reading a book, or nourishing and moving your body in ways that keep it healthy and full of the joys of life.

We now live in a digital age where technology is all around us. I've owned a smartphone since my early thirties, although I was quite late in acquiring one because I loved my retro flip phone. It's undoubtedly a key part of my professional life and has opened lots of doors for my career (not least, this book!). My smartphone helps me every day, whether it be navigating the best route into town, booking a taxi, or staying connected to my friends and family, and I'd struggle without it. I know I overuse it at times and have used it to escape from difficult feelings or distract myself from the more boring or challenging tasks I need to do. I know it's also sometimes made me feel bad that I haven't been as present with others as I feel I ought to have been, or that I've wasted a whole evening online doing nothing useful. I know I can do better, and I know many parents and adults feel this too.

The
Smartphone
Solution

Dr Martha Deiros Collado

The
Smartphone
Solution

Dr Martha Deiros Collado

Thorsons

Thorsons
An imprint of HarperCollins*Publishers*
1 London Bridge Street
London SE1 9GF

www.harpercollins.co.uk

HarperCollins*Publishers*
Macken House, 39/40 Mayor Street Upper
Dublin 1, D01 C9W8, Ireland

First published by Thorsons 2025

1 3 5 7 9 10 8 6 4 2

A catalogue record of this book is available from the British Library

ISBN 978-0-00-877392-2

Printed and bound in the UK using 100 per cent renewable electricity at
CPI Group (UK) Ltd

This book contains FSC™ certified paper and other controlled
sources to ensure responsible forest management.

For more information visit: www.harpercollins.co.uk/green

Contents

For the parents of today –

Who are doing things differently, even when it's hard.

I see you.

We can do this together.

Because here's the thing: parents don't just have to consider the risks and benefits of their own smartphone use, but also how they're going to handle the issue of smartphones with their children. Saying 'Not yet' to your child about getting a smartphone can be hard, as can teaching them how to stay safe while using one once they do. But as a psychologist and a parent of two small children, I have both professional and personal skin in the game. It's not quite time for me to have this conversation with my daughters yet (our eldest is six and our youngest has barely turned eighteen months old), but with each passing day I know I'm edging closer to questions like, 'When can I get a smartphone?' and 'How old do I have to be to have my own smartphone?' and things like, 'My cousin has got one, so why can't I have one too?' Looking at this through a professional lens, I can appreciate how difficult the pressure of getting your child a smartphone might seem when all their friends have one and they're missing out on conversations, which for teenagers are not just a 'good to know' but are essential to their sense of identity and belonging. And I hear the fears that giving unfettered access to the internet via a smartphones bring to parents, and how impossibly hard it can feel to be pushing back against the current teenage social tide.

At their core, all children have three basic needs: to be seen, to feel soothed and to feel safe. Children who feel seen have a sense of belonging – they feel comfortable being vulnerable and are more likely to develop emotionally secure relationships with others. Feeling soothed is about children developing emotional intelligence and healthy coping strategies to better navigate the challenges and stressors they might face. And feeling safe is about creating a haven in your home and the commitment not to be a source of fear or threat to your child, but instead to remain on their team when they get things wrong and make mistakes, and to apologise when you make mistakes too.

Letting your child use a screen might feel like you're meeting their needs in a quick and effective way; for example, stopping them from feeling boredom, frustration or irritability when waiting in a long queue at the Post Office. But their needs are only being met at a superficial level, which in turn can rupture an opportunity to build healthy self-regulation and to feel 'seen' in the real world. Whenever we use a screen to distract our children from their basic need to interact with us, their loving grown-ups, so we can just get on with our day, we inadvertently send a message that 'I can't give you my time, but I can give you a screen.' This might be necessary at times, and when it happens only occasionally then there's no harm done. But over time, if screens become your 'go-to' survival parenting tool, it's likely that they'll switch from TV to tablets to – eventually – smartphones. And if you've embedded the idea that screens can fulfil their most basic need, your time and presence, is it surprising that they might then lean on screens for fun, for connecting with others, for emotional soothing and relaxation, more than seeking out experiences with real people offline?

There's an underlying narrative of blame towards parents for their children using and owning smartphones. I've heard parents being called 'lazy' for giving children screens rather than giving them their presence and time, I've heard parents who use screens at mealtimes getting judged, and I've seen parents who sit on a bench receiving side-eye glares for staring at their phones while their child is coming down the slide. You can look back at your childhood and perhaps think, 'Thank goodness my parent never did that to me.'

This type of 'blame' narrative, however, undermines a fundamental truth of parenting. In every generation, adult brains have needed a break and some sort of distraction from parenting, not out of 'laziness' or 'bad parenting', but for something far more fundamental. Using a screen or smartphone as a 'surrogate' parent is something most parents have done in moments of need, and I can't claim that I'm guiltless in this regard. Whether it be at times when your child wants to play but you're in the middle of cooking, are trying to finish work for a tight deadline, need to grab a moment of peace before bedtime or feel the need to meet the expectation of presenting 'a good, quiet child'. In an adult world full of childism, where children's rights and needs are devalued in favour of adult interests and wants, it's happened. This doesn't make you a bad parent. It simply means you're a parent struggling with the load you've got to carry, and using screens is a coping strategy for survival. This is why I don't agree with the current narrative of 'blame', 'judgement' and 'shame' on parents. And that's without the fact that when we use blame, we remove responsibility and instead dish out shame. When a parent thinks, 'I am a bad parent', they are more likely to side-step the conversation and close off.

Instead, what we need to do as parents is to grow awareness and become more accountable. We must acknowledge how our collective actions as adults in modern society have impacted on the messages children receive about smartphones. We must accept that our behaviours make smartphones extremely desirable and highly rewarding, and that is why the relationship we have created with our smartphones is one we must change for the well-being of our children. We don't want to hear them say one day, 'You did this to me,' nor that they'd rather have had a relationship with a parent who didn't miss those small, irreplaceable moments in their childhood because they were on their phone. So we have to take this golden opportunity to learn and take different actions that can leave a lasting impact on the next generation.

Whether your child is not yet thinking about smartphones or has been begging you for one for months, pausing to notice your feelings about your child having a smartphone – shock, surprise, fear, sadness or anger – and accepting them as valid and important is a good first step. The key is neither to freeze and do nothing, nor to act out the strong feelings that have been sparked within your body when thinking about it. You should carefully consider the actions you want to take and the consequences of these actions, always being aware that your children are digital natives. Living in a healthy relationship with technology is something they must learn to do, not avoid. I believe with all my heart that parents are the solution to the smartphone dilemma, not the problem.

Most parents instinctively want to shield their children from experiencing pain, disappointment or feeling left out of their social groups. This is one of the main reasons parents give in to buying a first smartphone. The peer pressure that children – as well as adults – experience is very real, and it can leave adults feeling as if their only options are to buy their child a smartphone or ban them altogether.

I've written this book to offer you a third option, one that can do away with the power battle parents and children get trapped in, and mean that pleading, begging and relentless negotiations over smartphones don't even become a thing. In the first part of the book I'll help you understand what the research says about the risks and benefits of smartphones and give you my recommendation. In the second part we'll delve into this new, alternative option: a choice that invites your child to get on board with the idea of delaying smartphones from the get-go. When parents make this choice, it can feel empowering and supportive, and I provide you with tools you can use to stay grounded.

This third option is called the 'Family Phone Pledge Plan', and its seven steps form the core of this book:

- **Step 1: It starts with you.** It's how you live, not what you tell your children to do, that has the greatest impact on who they'll become. During this step we'll be reflecting on your values and your parenting style, and helping you set clear boundaries.
- **Step 2: Understanding your child.** Now that you understand yourself and your influence on your child a little more, let's look at who they are: their existing behaviours around tech, their temperament and when to worry.
- **Step 3: Open and honest dialogue.** In this step you will be offered scripts to help you talk about smartphones in ways that maintain your connection with your child. These will help you build a relationship of trust and give your child their greatest tool for protection, both online and offline – YOU.
- **Step 4: Join the Family Phone Pledge.** Learn how to construct your own Family Phone Pledge using the template, and engage the whole family in contributing and committing to it.

- **Step 5: Involving others.** Joining forces gives you the greatest chance of successfully embedding healthy smartphone habits in your home, so build a community around your Family Phone Pledge and encourage others to write their own. Develop strategies for when outside influences mean things don't go to plan.
- **Step 6: Find your SPARK.** Finding what works for you when it comes to living with a smartphone by considering: how you socialise and value face-to-face interactions more highly than the content of your phone, staying present for others even when your phone is around; the online apps and platforms you choose to access; the way in which you prioritise rest and sleep; and the skills and knowledge you model to your child when using your phone.
- **Step 7: Digital resilience.** Your child will eventually get a smartphone. In this last step of the Family Phone Pledge Plan, you'll learn to teach children digital skills that will help them stay safe online and know what to do when things go wrong. This part can feel unfamiliar and scary, but learning alongside your child is a beautiful thing to do.

I created the Family Phone Pledge Plan to help you strengthen the trust between you and your child, and give them a clear message – We are in this together. It's not about banning smartphones from your home, or saying, 'Never'. It's about saying, 'One day'. It's about using your parenting authority to open up a conversation about smartphones that's not a command. It's a gentle negotiation, an opportunity to build skills, so when the time comes, it feels right, it feels safer and you're both ready. And it's also about teaching your child that a smartphone is an incredibly powerful tool, and if they're going to carry a mini supercomputer in their pocket they need to do so with the understanding that it's not a status symbol or a toy, it's a responsibility.

I believe that when you lay the groundwork right from the start, with firm boundaries and open communication, it enables children to buy into your decision to delay smartphones while helping them to benefit from the period of waiting. It's just like children not being able to learn how to drive a car until they're seventeen. In the meantime, we begin to teach them road safety and encourage them to learn parts of the Highway Code as pedestrians – and backseat passengers – from an early age. Similarly, we can teach smartphone skills through our presence, words and actions in daily modelling with our own phones.

When you become a parent, you soon begin to realise that a lot of your day swings around the fine balance between finding your 'yes' and enforcing your 'no'. Toddlers need constant physical supervision, and this can feel exhausting and never-ending. As your child grows and develops, your daily dance doesn't end; it's only the types of behaviours you put into the 'yes' and 'no' box that look different. Depending on your parenting style, you may find it easier or harder to hold your 'no', enforce a limit and feel confident that you're doing the right thing. By the end of this book I want you to feel prepared and confident in the decision you make around smartphones, just as I hope you are about whether or not your child can have an ice lolly at breakfast. Whenever you say 'no' to smartphones, I want you to say 'yes' to more conversations about smartphones and 'yes' to more presence with your child, so that you can create more memories together, face to face in the real world. I want you to remember that saying 'not yet' to smartphones is not depriving your child, it's protecting their childhood. I want you to experience saying 'not yet' to smartphones as a necessary step on the road to building healthy lifelong habits. I want you to stay firm but kind, and for you to empathise with yourself as much as you do with your child during these smartphone-free years, so you can create family rules that bring you closer.

Our society is not going to become less digital, but we do have a choice about how we parent our children within it. Let's get started together.

Part One

The Wake-Up Call

If you're a parent, it's inevitable that you'll think about smartphones. Your child may not yet have a smartphone, but they might have used one – in or out of the home. I sometimes let my six-year-old daughter take photos or create videos to send out as virtual 'thank you' notes to friends and family after birthdays or Christmas. Wherever you are on this smartphone timeline, thinking about what to do with smartphones and how to 'get it right' feels critical right now.

The conversation around smartphones has become polarised, and understandably the language around them has sparked fear, anxiety and a sense of urgency to take rapid action to protect children. As a clinical psychologist, this tells me that adults care about children and want to protect their childhood, and these are both good things. However, fear is not an emotion that will help create sustainable and effective long-term solutions for our society, let alone ourselves, our children and our homes. Making sense of the research into smartphones, alongside reflecting on your parenting preferences, your child's needs and what's best for them developmentally, can help you look at this conversation with calm clarity and make choices that teach your child safe and healthy habits not just for now, but for life.

In Part One of this book I'll help you understand what the science says about the potential risks and benefits of smartphones, to give you an insight into this complex topic. But first I want to highlight an issue with current research. Without getting too deeply into this, it's a huge problem that current research focuses on screens, screen time, digital technology, smartphones, social media, instant messaging, the internet and going 'online' as if they are all interchangeable terms. Similarly, when we talk about children's mental health, studies look at levels of depression, anxiety, suicide, happiness, emotional distress and self-esteem in ways that suggest they're all equivalent measures of 'well-being'. But we simply can't say that the effect of smartphones on levels of depression is comparable to the effect of social media on levels of happiness. Many studies are not robust enough to validate or generalise an outcome because they're looking at very different things.

This all adds to the confusion and contradictory views among researchers and scientists in the field. Some research claims that the impact of smartphone use on well-being is complex and depends on individual characteristics, usage patterns and the context in which the device is used,[1] while others claim that teenagers with 'problematic smartphone use' are twice as likely to have symptoms of anxiety.[2] Where screen time is the number of minutes spent on a smartphone, some studies suggest there's a 'sweet spot' that's neither too much nor too little for young people, with no screen time having worse effects and moderate smartphone use being beneficial for overall well-being.[3] This is in contrast to studies that argue there is such a thing as 'too much screen time', and associates this with higher levels of anxiety and depressive symptoms in teenagers,[4] while systematic longitudinal studies show that the association between screen time and the prevalence of mental health problems in young people exists no matter how you look at it, but the correlation is so small that it can be deemed negligible.[5]

The reality is that science is constantly trying to catch up with the next area of concern because technology moves faster than humans can collect data. We have some solid research about screen time and online gaming, but when it comes to social media the picture is messy and unclear. Until more data can be gathered and the big tech giants agree to share the information they collect to feed into research (something we as a society should be urging them to give away freely), we'll continue to lack sufficient evidence to support something like a national ban. But when you have young children, waiting for the science to materialise is not an option. There's data we can usefully consider to help us make decisions that have a positive impact in our homes. Let's focus on children's core basic needs of feeling safe, seen and soothed, and look at how smartphones support or rupture this in relationship to us.

1

Safe

Should children be on screens at all?

One of the concerns around smartphones is that they are just adding another screen – and therefore further opportunities for screen time – into our children's lives. I think it's important to remember that not all screen time is equal. Although the simplest definition of screen time is 'the number of hours during which you use some sort of screen-based technology', three hours spent scrolling on a smartphone is very different to three hours spent as a family watching the latest film at the cinema. In fact, I'd like to suggest that it would be healthier and better for all concerned if families invested more time in watching TV together and parents offered children less individual time on devices such as a tablet or laptop that offer unfiltered access to the internet. And here's why.

The best data we have on screen time comes from research undertaken in the Adolescent Brain Cognitive Development (ABCD) study on nine- to ten-year-olds that took place over a period of two years.[1] Children and families reported screen time ranging from no time at all to over four hours a day. Screen time in this study included watching TV, films at the cinema, online videos and interactive pursuits like video games. The ABCD study monitored brain connectivity, physical health, mental health assessments and parental reports.[2] One of the unique features about this study was that experts in the field separate to the researchers checked the analysis plan for the data before it was carried out, adding an extra layer of rigour to the data.

The study outcomes showed that there was no meaningful association between time spent looking at a screen and levels of cognitive or mental health. Using screens for homework and learning, such as phonics, maths or writing, was shown to offer no greater harm or any less benefit than using old-school pen and paper. Moreover, screens were found to offer benefits to children (particularly those with a learning difficulty such as dyslexia), increasing their motivation and engagement, making work feel easier and enabling them to stay on track with their peers more successfully. This data is reassuring not only for our children but for ourselves too, if we're among the numerous adults who spend their working days glued to a screen.

Our children having screen time in itself is therefore not something we need to worry about, but we do know that looking at any kind of screen can become a distraction from the real world. Having said that, screens can be fun, entertaining and at times necessary to catch a break as a parent. As a child of the 1980s, the TV was often used as a babysitter for me, and I'm certainly not complaining about that. Our modern parental generation is using a lot less TV with children, and many families do not even own a TV at all. This to me is a great loss, because the alternative is usually to offer children a tablet, laptop or smartphone. A video online has not been created with children in mind in the same way as a children's TV show, with its dedicated team of producers, scriptwriters, artists and creators. You can't compare a child watching two episodes of *Bluey* to twenty minutes of watching an unboxing video online, nor is a family sitting together to watch a gameshow on a Saturday evening comparable to a child watching replays of video games on a tablet for an hour in their room. Watching a TV programme on a tablet or laptop isn't the concern. It's when they're being used for communication with others on virtual apps connecting children to one or many people that they become a different kind of tool, one that exposes children to the potential of viewing harmful content, including cyberbullying, violence, pornography and unrealistic standards of physical appearance, to name but a few.

There's no shame in needing twenty minutes to do a task without a child running around your feet or wanting a few minutes of peace and quiet and letting your child watch a screen. What matters is the kind of content your child is exposed to on that screen, and how much control over their safety you have while they're watching it. Ultimately, it's not screen time that's the concern, but how children use their screens.

We know that TV screen time is passive and can be less beneficial to children than interactive screen time (such as playing a video game, drawing on a tablet and so on), but TV offers adults greater control. Even if your TV has internet connectivity, it's unlikely to be the first port of call to access the internet in your family. This means that, by and large, what your child sees on a TV won't provoke the same level of concern as computers, tablets and smartphones.

Given that on average approximately a quarter of our waking hours are spent in front of a screen, it can be useful to take a few seconds to consider what screens you have in your home and how you spend time on them:

- Do you use them alone or with others?
- Are they used for work, fun, distraction or relaxation, or for something else altogether?
- Do you use screens together to enjoy or do something as a family?
- Which screens does your child or children have access to? Are these screens viewed alone or with others? Are they viewed for fun, work or for something else?

Whenever I question 'screen time' with my children, I find it reassuring to remember that it's not how much time a child spends watching a screen that impacts on their well-being; it's the distraction and diversion from opportunities to do things in the real world that matters. We often invite our eldest daughter to join us in the kitchen and make our family meal together, but there are evenings when we're running late, or she's tired, or we're just tired and want to cook without interaction, so we allow her to watch a couple of episodes of a TV show she enjoys for entertainment, which we know is not harming her or depriving her of other opportunities.

As parents, we can be mindful of not overusing screens as 'surrogate parents' that prevent our children from spending time with us, or become 'go-to' coping tools when things feel hard. And because it's relatively low-risk, TV can provide parents with an opportunity: because children have already begun a relationship with these screens years before they get a smartphone, we can practise embedding good tech habits before they get access to that turbo mini supercomputer in their pockets. In our home, we prioritise old-school TV cartoons, films and family shows that can bring joy, entertainment and a pause away from the busyness of life. I feel in control of what my children watch and we plan family screen time too; the aim is to ensure that it's not just passive – it's connecting and something we can talk about.

Reflect: what does screen time look like in your home?

Ask yourself the questions below and discuss them with anyone who has responsibility for your child, or discuss them with your child directly if they're over five years old and developmentally old enough to think about this with you.

1. Are you in control of the amount of screen time your child has? (i.e. have you set clear limits around how long they watch screens, and what they get to watch on them?)
2. Does watching screens interfere with the things you want to do as a family?
3. Are there protected spaces or activities that are 'screen-free zones'? (if the answer's 'no', could you consider any?)
4. Do screens interfere with sleep?
5. Are you in control of the snacks your child has available to them during screen time?

Please avoid comparing your answers with what others do. All families have different needs, and taking the time to pause and reflect on what works for you is the most important thing you can do. Working through these questions may help you see that you're already taking steps to protect family life outside of screens. If you feel happy with your answers, you can rest assured that you're probably doing as well as you can with the tricky issue of screen time. If you're not happy with the status quo or feel that you've lost control over screen time in your home, there are ways to set family limits and boundaries to help you put it in its place, such as protecting screen-free zones and putting your phone somewhere away from you. I'll be talking more about this in Part Two. The most effective strategies include setting time limits on screen use, creating a structure at weekends that avoids screens being used as a default and instead become an intentional tool for entertainment, making bedrooms 'screen free zones' and avoiding the use of screens during mealtimes as much as possible to avoid them interfering with bodily cues of fullness.

Smartphones: friend or foe?

There's a huge amount of fear about smartphones and the impact they can have on children's minds, their emotional well-being and their social relationships. Although many people believe that smartphones cause a 'dopamine kick' and that this can lead to addiction, in truth, anything you and I do that's pleasurable will give us a dopamine kick, because it indicates that we're experiencing pleasure. This could be watching a film or eating a pizza. Even if smartphones give us a dopamine kick, we've got no science to show it's any greater than anything else we do in life. Having said that, just because something isn't addictive doesn't mean it can't have a significant impact on our lives.

Smartphones follow a variable schedule of reinforcement,[3] which is the principle that gambling and lottery games are based on. What this means is that your behaviour on social media is rewarded in an unpredictable way; for example, the likes, shares and comments a post receives are rewards that follow no discernible pattern, and the notification icon and buzzing are an intermittent alert that can make you constantly check your phone just in case a new reward shows up. In other words, your phone can give you a short-term feelgood boost or immediate distraction from something in the real world that isn't as pleasurable or easy to cope with, such as the feeling of boredom.

Rather than feeling out of control with your phone, or seeing yourself as an unwitting victim of apps that are 'addictive by design', we can think about our relationship with smartphones as a form of compulsive behaviour that has developed from unhealthy habits we've unconsciously and automatically created. Smartphones are not addictive in themselves, but humans are by nature creatures of habit. The more we place blame on technology, the more likely we are to feel out of control with it and the more problematic and compulsive it will feel. Things like having an urge to check your phone, increasing symptoms of anxiety and worry about what's being posted on social media, feelings of fear or vulnerability when your phone isn't near you, and struggling to switch off, these can all be explained by understanding the process of habit formation. Let me explain how.

Habits form over time

Habits are created when we do things repeatedly in exactly the same way. When you first got a smartphone, it's likely that it took some time and effort to learn how to use it. For example, if you weren't brought up with mobile phones from an early age, you might have forgotten to take it with you or only picked it up when the ring sounded. Over time, however, you probably started adding apps, social media and text messaging platforms that made your phone buzz, beep and ring more frequently across the entire day (and night!). Checking your phone for new messages soon became habitual and you might have started using your smartphone at what were, at the time, unusual occasions, such as checking for school messages before breakfast or looking up news updates as you put together your child's packed lunches. You might also have started to hold on to it in situations where it gave you a sense of security, such as on the bus or while you walked home in the dark.

Smartphones as an inadvertent coping tool

Many people use smartphones for escapism or managing difficult emotions, such as sadness, anxiety and boredom. Research has shown that low self-esteem and low mood are predictors of greater smartphone and social media use. Going online can become habitual when we want to distract ourselves or need a coping strategy to deal with the problems and difficulties we experience in the real world. When smartphone use becomes a crutch that offers us emotional relief, we might be more likely to use our phone again without being consciously aware of doing so. Removing this coping tool can provoke feelings of stress and anxiety, because we now have to think on our feet about other ways of managing emotional discomfort. When this is a coping strategy that's become embedded in our daily lives and we then seek to address it, we'll have to sit with the discomfort of difficult emotions, boredom or that work task we've been procrastinating over. This can make many people twitchy as they fight the powerful urge to grab their phone.

Frequent behaviours embed habits

Just as habits form over time, the more frequently you check the phone, the more likely you are to embed this as a problematic habit.

Whether or not you experience these habits, as well as the extent to which they impact on your day-to-day living, is dependent on how aware you are of your phone use, and how the time you spend on it either aligns or is in conflict with your daily goals. If your level of self-reflection and self-regulation is low, then it's more likely that you'll be distracted by your smartphone throughout the course of the day.

Smartphones have done something clever: they use patterns of reinforcement that make habits stick faster and more strongly. The buzzing, sounds and lights that they produce have trained us to keep our phones close and respond to their calls. Thinking of our relation to smartphones as a form of addictive behaviour, however, demonises them and makes us think of them as dangerous technology. It's more helpful to think of them within the framework of habitual behaviour as this empowers us to consider both the positive and negative outcomes our choices with smartphones can bring. It also opens up space within which to think about what else – other than just relying on your phone – can help you when you experience uncomfortable feelings, want to distract yourself from the real world or need a distraction for entertainment. Although you might have developed bad habits with your phone, with the apps having trained you to compulsively check for more content, you can learn to change this and build better, more positive habits that impact not just you and your child or children, but all those around you. We'll talk more about how to do this on page 197.

Smartphones as portals to the internet

For a long time, many of us have deemed online risks to be less harmful than real-life, physical dangers. When you see your child holding a tablet on the sofa, you can at least be assured that they're physically safe in the warmth of your home. But we're beginning to wake up to the reality that going online presents risks that absolutely require our focused attention. Just as most parents wouldn't feel comfortable letting their eight-year-old spend two hours at the playpark completely unsupervised by a responsible and loving adult, we now know that it's unwise to let children spend two hours on the sofa using a smartphone that offers them unfiltered access to online content and contact with people that they've never met. We parents aren't concerned about smartphones because they're phones, but because the internet and social media grant unsupervised access to the wider world.

The risk of cyberbullying, sexually explicit content, unrealistic body standards, violence, grooming, and harmful content relating to suicide and self-harm has become a constant worry for parents whose children go online. It's important to remember that to grab an opportunity one must, more often than not, also accept an accompanying risk. To make a new friend online there's always going to be the danger of meeting someone with ill intentions, just as engaging with useful and educational content online – including things like the CBeebies website – can mean sharing personal information about yourself. To connect with real-world friends on a social networking site, you must be willing to give your name and age, and to search for useful advice about sexual health you must accept that you might encounter pornographic content because of the search terms you're going to key in. We must also reluctantly recognise as parents that children can be perpetrators of harm online just as much as they can be the targets of it.

A comprehensive analysis of potential online opportunities and risks for children offers an excellent summary of how they overlap:[4]

Online opportunities	Online risks
Access to global information	Illegal content
Shared experiences and peer support	Grooming, talking to strangers
Social networking among friends	Cyberbullying, trolling, hate comments
Entertainment, games, fun	Harmful and offensive content
Educational resources	Racist and hate material
Civic or political participation	Advertising and stealth marketing
User-generated content-creation	Abuse of personal information
Career progression/employability	Gambling/phishing/financial scams
Personal/health/sexual advice	Self-harm (suicide, pro-anorexia, bigorexia)
Specialist groups/fan forums	Invasion or abuse of privacy
Technological expertise/literacy	Illegal activities (hacking, copyright infringements)
Privacy for identity expression	Misinformation and fake news

This table is a useful reminder that the content found on the internet can be both brilliant and terrible, something that is worth remembering whenever we venture on social media or consider our children exploring the internet.

Although existing studies on social media are almost exclusively weak, inconclusive, and weighed down by a lack of quality information and conflicting evidence, and even though we cannot yet say which app or platform carries the greatest risk and which is the safest, some of the data we do have constitutes a useful guide to support our decisions as parents. Let's look at it now.

First, carrying out research about the impact of social media platforms isn't straightforward because unlike watching TV, it's impossible to predict precisely what children will see on social media ahead of time. Perhaps it will be a video about make-up or a new dance craze, or maybe it will be sexually explicit content, or information about self-harm or suicide. There are major issues surrounding academic research looking at online platforms, the main one being that there isn't a single, widely accepted definition of what 'social media' actually is. This raises numerous questions about what exactly is being investigated when we look at children's behaviour online. Is the impact of children seeing posts from people they know or don't know the same? Does it matter in terms of research analysis if children access sites where they're allowed to post or where they just have access to view? Do multiplayer games count as social media? What about dating apps or group messaging platforms such as WhatsApp, where children might get contacted in groups with people they've never met in person – do all or any of these count as 'social media', or are they in some way different?

Thinking about these questions isn't easy and, as a parent, the lack of clarity around them can often inspire difficult feelings. Despite the lack of studies and the frequently imprecise data, we can use our instincts as parents to guide us where the research does not. In the same way that I wouldn't let my child venture off to someone's home whom I don't know in person and whose address is unknown to me, I cannot justify allowing them to visit online spaces where I've no idea what they'll see, who they'll talk to or what they'll do once they get there.

Data collected from TikTok in 2022 by an American organisation called The Center for Countering Digital Hate (CCDH) reported that the site's algorithm recognised vulnerability in each person who accessed the platform.[5] Rather than seeing vulnerability as a signal to act with caution, the algorithm used it to its advantage to pull someone in to the digital world for longer. For example, the CCDH report found that when girls set up an account on TikTok, it took less than three minutes for them to be shown content on self-harm, eight minutes for content on eating disorders to come up, with videos about body image and mental health being recommended every thirty-nine seconds. When it came to boys, misogynistic and pornographic content was shown within three minutes of an account being set up. There are three important points to take from this:

1. As parents we cannot be blind to the content children have the potential to see when they have unfiltered access to the internet.
2. Social media taps into pre-existing vulnerabilities, making some children more vulnerable to harmful content than others. This idea is backed up by research that shows that children who struggle with mental health problems spend more time online than those who do not.
3. Social media was never created with children's well-being or safety in mind. It's a profitable business to extract information and data from us, the people who choose to use it.

Australia recently agreed a proposal to ban social media from November 2025 for under-sixteens. At first glance this sounds like an idea that should be implemented throughout the world to protect children when going online, but when you look a little deeper, it's not quite so simple. As we've seen, exactly what constitutes 'social media' hasn't been agreed – YouTube has been spared from the ban and Snapchat is trying to wiggle its way out.

YouTube is by far the most popular site for children and young people, with data showing 95 per cent of all teenagers use it, with 20 per cent reporting they do so 'almost constantly'. YouTube is a video-sharing platform with an age-rating of thirteen, but because there's no need to create an account to access the site, anyone of any age can access most of its content. In addition, there are no restrictions to uploading videos, which may put young children at risk of others discovering personal information about them online, such as seeing them in their school uniform. After watching any video, YouTube will suggest another video to watch, and sometimes these will play automatically. Because the algorithm prioritises engagement over content quality, it can steer children towards extreme content, even when they were initially watching an age-appropriate video.

In 2020 TikTok was fined $12.7 million by the US Federal Trade Commission after finding 1.4 million children under the age of thirteen were accessing its content without parental consent, and $5.7 million for the same thing in 2019. In 2023 they were fined £12.7 million by the British Information Commissioner for illegally processing the data of 1.4 million children under thirteen who were using its platform without parental consent. We now know that TikTok and most social media platforms haven't installed measures to detect or prevent children under thirteen to use the app, but they will track and profile children, including advertising to them and delivering harmful and inappropriate content at their very next scroll. To me as a parent, this says loud and clear that first, social media doesn't care about the safeguarding of children, and second, social media makes so much money that being fined a few million is meaningless. Now, consider the fact that YouTube also uses an algorithm and is the most used platform by young people, and the thought that it has slid past the proposed ban in Australia suddenly feels problematic.

As with any drastic proposals, there are going to be issues with a reactive national ban of the type that Australia proposes to implement. There's no evidence base to support its blanket-ban decision, which many have argued will isolate children, particularly those who live in physically remote and marginalised communities (which in a country as big as Australia might have some dire consequences), deprive young people of the positive aspects of connecting on social media, discourage children from reporting harm when they experience it online and put young people at greater risk of accessing the dark web. It also reduces the pressure for platforms to improve online safety for all. Personally, I ground myself in the knowledge that social media was never created for children and I choose to exercise my parental authority to set safe boundaries around it. We don't have to let our children be exposed to content that's inappropriate or harmful to them, and we should see it a worthy use of our parenting role to stay informed and be aware of the 'digital diet' our children are consuming.

Empowering ourselves as parents is imperative, particularly when you consider that many of these 'ban' proposals contain loopholes that tech companies will try to exploit. Let's look at Snapchat, which is currently trying to wriggle out of the Australia ban by arguing that it's a messaging platform like WhatsApp, rather than a social media app. Snapchat is the second-most popular platform used by teenagers, with its biggest pull being the disappearing message feature, where images vanish after a few seconds. The minimum age to use Snapchat is thirteen, but there are very few checks to stop children accessing the platform at any age. The National Society for the Prevention of Cruelty to Children (NSPCC) reported an 82 per cent rise in online grooming crimes against children in the last five years, with 73 per cent involving Snapchat as the communication tool used by perpetrators to initiate contact with children. The app's lack of parental controls makes it impossible for parents to have a handle on who their children are interacting with and what kind of conversations they're having. For some adults, the idea of disappearing images appears safer than an app where photos and images leave a permanent digital footprint, such as Instagram. This type of app, however, poses greater potential risks: users can still screenshot content, it's impossible to trace where the content has come from, and it's a lot easier to surprise children with distressing and violent content over which they have no control.

Social media wasn't specifically created for children, and we've seen how the opportunities it offers are intertwined with manifold potential risks. As a parent, if you feel anxious about letting your child access social media on a smartphone, your concern is legitimate and quite understandable. Empowering ourselves with knowledge about what lies within these apps is key to enabling us to think about the choices we make, where we let our children spend their digital time and what we need to do to curate an online experience that's safe for them. Our parenting power lies in education and connection, not just restriction and control.

On social media, children are not just dealing with content; they're also faced with comparison, shame and validation anxiety. We must teach them that their worth isn't found in how many 'likes' they get or how many comments they receive, and we need to empower them to develop the skills to deal with rejection, mean comments, bullying and distressing videos. Before they possess these skills, going on social media is unlikely to offer many beneficial opportunities but it may place children at risk of harm, so we need to stop parenting from the sidelines and have the courage to lead from the front. We can protect and prepare – both can go hand in hand.

What are the risks to mental health?

Children are not mini adults. Their brains are still developing and they need a diverse menu of experiences for them to flourish, including allowing their minds to get bored and their imaginations to wander into worlds of make-believe at will. Unlike mature adult brains, children's brains are able to suspend time and focus their full attention on a moment in the here and now. This is an extreme version of mindfulness, where past events, future tasks and environmental noises disappear when children are fully engrossed in a pleasurable activity of their choice. This can make children appear to be in a dreamlike state, one that can feel frustrating to many parents (because it appears their ears get switched off!).

It is, however, a key part of development and one of the reasons why smartphones can lure children in more than adults. The constant stream of notifications, information, moving and engaging content that exists on smartphones attracts their attention and can make it difficult for them to focus or attend to other tasks. The prefrontal cortex, our brain's centre of self-control, which mediates impulses, memory, focus and attention, doesn't mature until our mid-twenties, which is why children and adolescents have poor impulse control. This makes them more vulnerable to following their curiosity online, opening apps that are inappropriate or watching content that is way beyond their emotional maturity.

In short, a young brain lacks a fully developed self-control system to help them stop the compulsive behaviour of constantly checking their phone. It's also the reason why children get over-stimulated so much faster with a smartphone than adults, which is often witnessed as meltdowns, irritability or tearfulness when they're asked to switch off their tablet, TV or laptop, if they have access to one. You can learn to watch out for and mitigate these so-called 'phone flags', which I will discuss in Chapter 3.

The research agency Childwise interviewed 2,200 children aged between five and sixteen, and among their findings were that children get their first phone as young as seven years old and that owning a smartphone becomes almost universal at age eleven.[6] YouTube is accessed every day by 61 per cent of young people who own a smartphone, followed by Snapchat, TikTok, Instagram and WhatsApp, although the top-five order is forever changing. I have friends with children in Year 6, and every single child in the classroom has a smartphone; some parents I see in therapy have told me that their nine-year-olds are excluded from playtime with their friends because they're among the only ones without a phone.

Understanding the risks matters, because the fear that social media might impact upon children and young people's mental health is both entirely reasonable and commonly held. Unease about the internet chimes with many people's personal experience online, particularly when videos, comments or personal messages make us feel intense emotions. However, we so far have no scientific data to demonstrate that social media has a negative impact on young people's mental health. Social media has been shown to contribute to 0.36 per cent of the covariance in depressive symptoms in teenage girls, and to 0.01 per cent of the covariance in depressive symptoms in teenage boys.[7] In lay terms, this means that time spent on social media cannot be reliably used to predict any changes in depressive moods that young people experience. A meta-analysis in 2021 of thirty-seven studies looking at social media and smartphones' influence on mental health outcomes in young people concluded that given the current body of good data, 'there is no evidence that social media contributes to suicidal ideation or other mental health outcomes'.[8]

The uncomfortable truth is twofold: first, that current research in this area is sloppy yet often stated overconfidently, and second, that mental health is incredibly complex. In order to look at the true impact of social media on young people's mental health, good research must account for variables that impact on mental health from the outset. This includes factors such as socioeconomic status, race, unemployment rate, family dynamics, previous trauma, health and social relationships. Most studies don't do this, or only account for one or two variables at most. This means that rather than their findings offering insight into the impact of social media on young people's mental health, they instead might be highlighting something else.

Amy Orben has dedicated the last ten years to researching the impact of social media on young people's mental health and has won multiple awards for her 'gold standard' research. She found that a small positive correlation between social media use and measures of anxiety and depression are most likely a reflection of young people's mental health experiences, rather than solely caused by going on social media. In other words, young people who experience greater anxiety and low mood are likely to spend more time on social media watching content that reinforces their current mental health state. This is important information for parents to help make sense of how vulnerable their child might be to the effects of social media and can offer clues about the mental health of those who overuse smartphones or struggle to come off them.

Indeed, some studies suggest that young people's online worlds are mirrors of their in-person experiences. A paper in the *Lancet*, a medical journal that publishes original research on clinical, public and global health, reported data from over 120,000 young people and found that 90 per cent of children who experienced cyberbullying were also targets of bullying offline, and that this 'traditional' bullying was more insidious.[9] Research consistently shows that cyberbullying and traditional bullying overlap, and cyberbullying is often a continuation of existing bullying behaviours. What is clear is that bullying is opportunistic – the less a child is protected or supervised, the more likely it is to occur. This is as true for traditional bullying as it is for the online variety.

Once children own a smartphone, it's a bigger challenge for parents to monitor what they're accessing online. The responsibility therefore lies with adults to advocate for the safety and well-being of children, and to support, guide and protect them. If you know your child has tricky relationships with friends and peers at school, be aware that these interactions are likely to get amplified online; in such cases, rather than a smartphone helping your child socialise and connect with others, it might make them easier targets for online bullying.

Most studies ignore the opinions of young people in the research itself, and it was therefore a welcome relief to find the Boston Children's Digital Wellness Lab survey that studied 1,480 young people from a broad diverse of backgrounds aged between thirteen and seventeen.[10] When they were asked about the positive and negative impact of social media, 49.9 per cent reported that social media made friendships better, and the vast majority reported social media made them feel socially connected (79.4 per cent) and emotionally supported by peers (69 per cent) sometimes, often or always. Precisely half of those surveyed reported never or rarely feeling lonely or isolated, while 54.9 per cent felt sad or depressed and 48.6 per cent that their life was worse than other people's. However, young people in the study did report that social media interfered with sleep, time with family and impacted on their academic grades (31.3 per cent), and had a negative impact on their body image (46 per cent).

When children engage online, it's not as simple as getting them to access only the sites or activities we approve of because, as we saw from the table on page 28, the opportunities are inextricably linked with the risks. Even though the jury is out about whether social media has an impact on mental health, we do still need to go forward with our eyes open. Rather than looking at mental health as the only factor that gets affected, we need to be asking, 'What's happening to our children when they spend time on a smartphone in terms of their cognitive, social and emotional development?'

As with most things, there's likely to be a mix of positives and negatives, but for now we can rely on the fact that social media wasn't created for children and should be used by no one younger than thirteen years old. We need to open our awareness to the fact that children and young people have an innate curiosity to explore apps and sites beyond their years. This can inadvertently propel them towards unanticipated negative experiences for which their young minds and hearts may be unprepared, and where their capacity to cope will be pushed beyond their abilities. In the same way that you might protect your children from viewing a programme with an age rating of 15 until they're ready to do so, it's reasonable and justifiable to protect your child from accessing social media until their brain is mature enough to cope with the seductive digital pursuits it offers. Furthermore, you shouldn't dismiss the negative impacts that accessing social media can have on family cohesion and experiences, sleep and academic performance; young people are aware of these impacts and raise them as a concern.

Reflect: what are your smartphone hopes and fears?

Get a piece of paper and draw three columns: one for 'hopes', a second for 'risks' and a third for 'actions'. Write down the hopes and fears you have for your child having a smartphone to:

1. spend time on social media sites
2. connect with others through calls/texts/messaging apps
3. do research and explore the internet

Now consider your hopes and fears for your child in the real world to:

1. attend a club or activity where you are not present to supervise
2. go to a sleepover at a friend's house
3. get from A to B on public transport/trusting where they are and who they are with

Once you've made a list, think about the third column. What actions do you need to take for your child to experience more of the hopes (opportunities) and less of the fears (risks)? Are there skills or information you need to teach your child? What resources, knowledge or skills do you need to do this? Do you need to invite others – such as parents, family and friends – to join you to make this possible?

You might like to repeat this activity with your child, inviting them to list their hopes and fears for getting a smartphone as above. You could then share your list with them. This might lead you to a gentle introduction into discussing smartphones, with perhaps the beginning of some shared actions to think about together.

Smartphones and physical safety

We've discussed the impacts of smartphones, social media and online content on children's emotional safety, but it's often argued that having a smartphone can enhance their physical safety.

This is a common argument I hear from parents who are concerned about keeping their children safe, particularly when they're apart for long periods of time, whether as a result of travel, family separation, illness or work circumstances.

It makes sense to think that carrying a smartphone keeps children safer because they can easily be reached by a quick call (assuming, that is, that they've not set it to silent). Carrying an expensive piece of kit such as a smartphone, however, can also put children in a more vulnerable position, as statistics relating to theft, mugging and physical attacks brutally illustrate. A UK Home Office study reported in 2023 that 70 per cent of all thefts in London were related to mobile phones. Children and young people are disproportionately targeted. Whereas there is a 1 per cent chance of an adult being threatened for their mobile, the risk rises to 5 per cent for those aged eleven to sixteen years old. It's easy to spot who has a phone on the street, with a quarter of all phone robberies involving somebody using their phone or having it on display. Manufacturers and the tech industry have a responsibility to reduce opportunities for criminals to benefit from the resale of stolen handsets, but until they choose to take drastic measures in this regard, it's down to us – the children's loving grown-ups – to offer protection.

There are a few precautions you can teach your child, including keeping their phone safe and out of sight when they're walking or travelling (i.e. not texting or calling on the go), being aware of their surroundings at all times and knowing how to report any incident to the police. These precautions are just as important for adults to follow, but the key difference for me is that children are more readily distracted, especially when they're out and about with friends, and they're also a lot more vulnerable. The reason they get targeted more is because the younger they are, the easier it is to threaten them.

I've met a couple of young boys who've been mugged, both of them on a tube platform in London, and although they were lightly injured, they were deeply shaken emotionally. It's never a child's fault when incidents like these happen. Robberies are most often opportunistic, and in the great scheme of things they're still relatively rare. But the question remains, is it necessary to put children at risk when there are other types of phone on the market, such as a standard so-called 'brick' phone like the Nokia 105? These are widely available and can just as easily make calls and send texts, but they lack the high-value appeal that smartphones offer criminals.

Another way in which parents might believe they can protect their child's physical safety by allowing them to have a smartphone is because they can track their whereabouts and keep a safe eye on them. I totally get the appeal of tracking. My friends and I have had our tracking switched on at festivals to locate each other more easily without needing to call or message, and I've got my tracking switched on when I go running at night so my husband can see where I am. It definitely helps me feel safer. In both instances tracking is being used with open and clear communication, and for a time-limited period. I choose when I'm happy to be tracked, and I can switch the function off when I want to. When it comes to monitoring children's whereabouts, however, I think it can often do more harm than good.

In my experience, parents typically switch on tracking as a non-negotiable, with children getting punished and their phones removed if they ever switch it off. Despite such parental faith in the system, research shows that tracking offers a false sense of safety to parents and that it can erode trust in the relationship they have with their child.[11] When children feel like their privacy is being invaded, it undermines their sense of mutual honesty and leads to greater conflict, making children more likely to do things behind their parents' back and less likely to turn to their parents for help when things go wrong.

Children are highly tech savvy, and bypassing tracking doesn't require a lot of skill. Children can disable location features, leave their phone in safe locations and use clever apps to trick the trackers. Using a non-smartphone wearable device such as a GPS watch brings the same issues, and it's been reported that some companies may be collecting and selling user data, which can pose security risks, given that real-time and historical data, as well as personal details, are being recorded. More importantly, just because a child says they're somewhere doesn't mean they're doing what they've said. As children get older and their lives become more separate to those of their loving parents, it's a steep learning curve of teaching responsibility, building trust, letting go, and coming safely back together to talk, re-tell experiences and problem-solve as needed. Using a tracker on a smartphone might tell you where your child is, but it doesn't teach your child how to make good decisions while they're away from you. That can only be learnt in relationship and through open communication with you. Rather than relying on tracking, work on teaching your child how to make safe, age-appropriate decisions, and build a relationship of trust that tells them you'll be there to support them no matter what. When you feel your child is ready to spend more time away from you, then you can allow them to take what will feel like 'safe risks' away from you.

There may be times, however, when your child asks to be tracked or perhaps wants to track your whereabouts too, and they might even use this as an argument for why they should have a smartphone. If this happens, it's about having an open conversation about the possible benefits of such an arrangement, why tracking might give them a sense of safety and what else could help keep them feeling safe at times when they want to know you're close, even when you're apart. It's something I do with my husband from time to time, and it's always worth comparing the real risks of an activity such as running on your own in the dark with possible alternatives, such as joining a running group. Ultimately, it's always better to keep lines of communication open with your child and develop tools to cope with the big feelings that show up in you and them about their growing independence, rather than rely solely on a location app.

2

Seen

All children have a fundamental need to be seen. This isn't just about eye contact, it's about 'seeing' your child as a way of knowing, understanding and noticing who they are, which is fundamental to the development of their positive self-esteem, self-worth and confidence.

It's the reason little ones spend so much time shouting, 'Look at me!' in an attempt to make you see what they're doing, even when it's something like spinning around, which looks like a fairly pointless action to you. What your child is truly trying to say is 'Please notice me!' and this is essential to help them develop a sense of who they are. 'Seeing' your child means understanding what they like and what they don't like, what they find easy and what's a struggle, to notice what they do and say . . . not all the time, but enough times to give them the sense that you enjoy being with them, that you value their unique character and 'see' them as individuals in their own right.

This might be an effort for most parents because it means concentrating on your child in the 'here and now', something that our adult brains struggle to do as our patterns of thinking tend to project us into the future and the next task, meaning that simply 'being' with a child can feel exhausting and oftentimes boring. The temptation to look at your phone at such times might be strong, and learning to recognise how this takes your presence away and the impact it might have on your relationship with your child is important. When we take the time to 'see' our children, they begin to see something valuable and worthwhile in themselves too.

Children also need to feel seen in social contexts with their peers. As they grow up and develop friendships, feeling seen within a peer group is important for their sense of belonging, and their teenage years in particular are a critical time for being seen and developing a sense of self.

The double-edged sword of socialising

To be human is to be social. We have a profound need to socialise with others for our survival and well-being. Nonetheless, it takes a lot of brain power to communicate with words, make sense of non-verbal language, and dim down all the environmental noises that surround us in order to understand social meaning and respond in an articulate way. Socialisation takes much more effort for young ones, as they're learning the foundation of social skills and their brains are still developing. This is why children are often exhausted after school, and the reason behind those meltdowns, irritability and tears after a high-energy birthday party, an exciting day out or a family get-together. Adults often blame such behaviour on sugary foods, but the truth is that the more people a child interacts with, the more brain power they have to use. Children's brains need to have time to decompress, rest and recharge, in ways that allow them to switch off.

I was recently speaking to a twelve-year-old I know about what she does on her phone. She told me that she listens to music, plays games, sends messages and makes calls to her parents. That was it. It sounded simple and clean, until she shared how overwhelming it was to be on WhatsApp. She said she'd decided to come off all group chats because the family rule is to switch off phones after 6 p.m., meaning that every morning she had hundreds of messages that she never managed to catch up on. Now, different children will approach socialising online in their own particular way, just as they do in the real world. This is a sensible twelve-year-old who of her own accord chose to delete WhatsApp and only use standard text messages on a one-to-one basis. But how many children would struggle to do this and, rather than delete WhatsApp, choose to stay up through the night to read all the messages so as not to have FOMO (fear of missing out)?

When it comes to socialising, we can have too much of a good thing. One of the unexpected outcomes of smartphones is that although they give us the tools to socialise with more people, the socialising we do is more superficial and less meaningful. British anthropologist Robin Dunbar proposed what's become known as 'Dunbar's number', which suggests we can only have a maximum of 150 meaningful relationships across our lifespan. Of these, only five are deemed to be people we love deeply, fifteen are close friends with whom we spend regular time, fifty are friends we enjoy spending time with, and the rest are acquaintances that we may have met a few times.

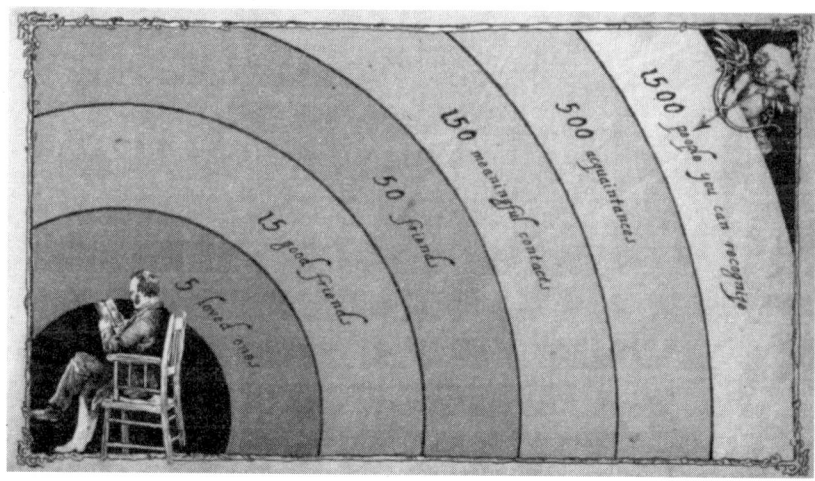

Dunbar's number is a theory that's widely used but has been criticised for being founded on the premise that our brain's architecture defines the size of our social networks. It's likely someone can love more than five people or have more than fifteen meaningful friendships. Thinking that the numbers suggested by Dunbar are wholly accurate is possibly best avoided, but the idea that having more than 150 meaningful relationships is a difficult commitment for someone to make isn't hard to believe. If we now think back to smartphones and the many contacts it's easy to accrue on social media and messaging apps, it's simple to see how quickly a young teen can end up with hundreds if not thousands of messages on group chats. Because children don't communicate the way adults do, with intention, but rather chat online as they would do offline about a million topics that feel pertinent and important in that instant, the message overload quickly builds up.

As children's brains develop, children seek greater acceptance and recognition from their peers. Smartphones can amplify the need to be seen, as children may feel pressure to stay 'switched on' so they don't miss a beat. Smartphones can help children stay up to date with the latest trends, memes and challenges, which can help them fit in with their peers. Being a part of messaging groups can foster a sense of belonging and connection, while also offering children a platform on which to express their creativity and identity through photos, videos and posts. But because children's brains are in development, still learning the nuances and complexities of social interaction, the influx of online messages can be such a massive sensory overload that it sends their brain and nervous system out of control, and leads to a rise in anxiety.

Are smartphones making us lonely?

Even if teenagers do manage to keep up with what can be an overwhelming amount of communication, is it enriching their lives or, conversely, making them more isolated? A number of studies and reports show that most people use their smartphone to text and send messages rather than make calls, with the average teenager sending fifty text messages a week.

For children and young people, texting can seem really attractive because it removes all of the awkwardness of interacting with people face to face. The child who feels shy during new encounters no longer stands out in a group chat in which all people see is words on a screen, not shaky whispers uttered with a lack of eye contact. It's a lot easier as a young teenager to find your voice and have an identity free of awkwardness online than in real life. This also explains why children with neurodivergent brains prefer to communicate via texts and smartphones. It's slower-paced and removes a lot of the sensory stimulation of face-to-face interaction, where facial expressions, non-verbal communication through gestures, environmental noises and other stimuli take a lot of brain power to filter.

But when we primarily connect with others via written messages, we miss out on the opportunity to hear another person's tone of voice, emotional expression, and whether they have a cold or sound croaky – all those small inflections that make each of us human, and bring something personal and real to each moment of physical interaction. It's vastly different to text someone a cancellation when you cannot make a commitment you agreed to rather than calling them to apologise, or sending a birthday meme as compared with getting a 'Happy Birthday!' phone call. Researchers measured levels of cortisol – the hormone responsible for our stress response – in college students just before their final exams.[1] They found that those who received a supportive text message from their mother had no reduction in their levels, whereas those who received a supportive phone call from their mothers did show a decrease. Interestingly, students who engaged in a FaceTime call with audio and video had a markedly significant lowering of cortisol levels and a rise in oxytocin, the feel-good hormone.

This simple study powerfully illustrates that the antidote to stress is human connection, and smartphones can bring us closer to each other by enabling us not just to hear the voice of those we love but to see them in real time, which can have a major impact on our physiological state. But when we only send texts, smartphones can cause a big disconnect. It might be fine to send text messages when we're doing something functional, such as asking a question or setting a time to meet. When it comes to managing meaningful relationships, however, texting might actually leave us feeling more disconnected. And we know that feeling social disconnection is the route to loneliness, which is associated with an increased risk of depression, anxiety and health-related conditions including heart disease, strokes and premature death. As human beings we're primed to be social, and experiencing loneliness is like suffering from an unquenchable thirst. Loneliness is a signal from our body that we're lacking something that we need for survival, and if we can seek out and find meaningful connection we can thrive again.

There's a widely held stereotype that loneliness is more prevalent among older adults who are isolated, and this can of course happen. But loneliness affects those of all ages, and a recent experiment involving 55,000 people showed that higher levels of loneliness were present among young people across cultures, countries and genders, with 14 per cent of ten- to twelve-year-olds and 11 per cent of thirteen- to fifteen-year-olds reporting feeling lonely.[2] Loneliness is not the same as being alone. Although children are constantly surrounded by peers of the same age, they sometimes have poor relationships with them and don't always feel connected. And despite children aged ten to fifteen being the group that tend to begin to own smartphones and may therefore be connected with peers digitally, on the whole they prefer texting over other forms of communication because it's fast and easy, more private than a phone call on which parents might eavesdrop, gives them extra time to formulate a response, and removes the awkwardness of talking and showing emotions. Children's vulnerability to loneliness, coupled with their preference for texting, might be amplifying and escalating rates of depression, anxiety and other mental health problems that we know are risk factors of loneliness.[3]

We must all become aware that socialising via text or instant messages is not offering us the meaningful connections we crave. A quick text message can be useful when you have something quick to say or respond to, like an invitation to meet up with friends, but it might be time to consider sharing a little more of ourselves, accept the awkwardness, tolerate the cringe, and start making more phone calls and video calls, or get into using voicenotes. It's important to recognise that the essence of what makes us human gets lost when we connect primarily via texts. If we want to teach our children that phones can be useful tools for connection, let's allow them the experience of being with each other, whether it's a call, a video or, best of all, in person.

Reflect: how do you socialise, and with whom?

Take a few moments to think about who your friends are. Put them in columns as per Dunbar's diagram. Consider the people you'd share information about something personal with, perhaps details of a minor surgical operation, or the friends that you'd want to share your pregnancy with in person outside of your family circle. They're your 'good friends'. Now consider who else you are friends with that you appreciate spending time with and see regularly enough that you have an easy, flowing conversation even when time since you last saw each other has passed. These people are your 'friends'. And finally, have a think about those you are friendly with and enjoy seeing but might not see as often or have a less intimate connection with, who you wouldn't as easily share something personal with. These are your meaningful contacts.

Think about how you socialise with each of these groups of people. Who do you tend to see more face to face? Who do you spend more time texting or messaging online? How does the way you socialise with them reflect the closeness of your relationship, if at all?

It can be helpful to reflect on how you interact with those you want to have meaningful relationships with and the ways in which you're modelling connection with others to your children. Are you happy with the status quo or are there small actions you can take to create closer bonds with those that are important to you? How are the ways you use your phone to connect with others modelling to your child the kinds of connection you'd like them to prioritise in the future?

Technoference

When I was a teenager, brick phones appeared, with the ability to take and make calls on the go and very basic messaging. My father was one of the first people I knew who had a brick phone, and he used it solely for work. I remember this huge, unsightly rectangular thing being carried around everywhere. He was glued to it at all times and I bought him a chocolate bar in the shape of a mobile phone for his birthday as a joke. I remember walking on a beautiful beach at sunset while on holiday with my parents and my mother hurling his brick phone into the sea. He had dared to respond to a work call.

My dad was – and still is – what most people would define as a workaholic, and the problem with this, particularly as a child, is that you don't feel like you can compete with your parent's obsession. No child wants to be a burden who pulls their mum or dad away from something that provides them with essential needs, such as food, shelter, toys and pleasurable activities like holidays. My father didn't have a smartphone back then because they didn't exist, but the end result was the same – his phone took him away from being present with his family. For many, work is necessary to provide and subsist. And we need to be conscious that work can at times also be a welcome distraction that takes us away from family life, and phones are tools that make switching off from the mundane, stressful and chaotic parts of parenting so much easier.

I'm not having a go at my father for his behaviour. We're much closer now that I'm an adult and parent too, and he's aware of how his work impacted our family. But I'm also not blaming the brick phone for doing what it was supposed to do – keep him connected to his work. I want to bring awareness to the choices you and I and anyone who owns a phone make in everyday life while in the presence of others, and how this interferes with other people's essential need to feel seen. The strong message that removing yourself from a real-life situation, feeling or interaction sends to those you're with is that whatever is on your phone is more important than the people who surround you. It's really easy to blame smartphones for pulling our attention towards them, but how honest are we about the choices we make?

We've got a word for the experience of allowing technology to interfere with our lives: 'technoference'. We've also got one for the act of ignoring someone when you grab your phone in front of them: 'phubbing', a shorthand version of 'phone snubbing'. It's likely you'll have experienced phubbing and that you'll have probably done this at times to others too, often without the excuse of work, which can make phubbing feel more legitimate and pressing. You know the feeling: you sit across the table from someone, looking forward to spending a bit of time together, maybe catching up on their latest news, and just after you've put your coat over the back of your chair and settled into your seat, they put their hand in their pocket, pull out their phone and start scrolling. How does this make you feel? How does this feeling influence what you think about this person you were hoping to spend time with? How does it influence what you think about yourself in your relationship with them? You won't be surprised to hear that studies have found that phubbing leads to feelings of rejection, creates conflict and leads to greater unhappiness between couples.[4]

As parents and adults, we need to be aware of how our behaviour unwittingly impacts our children and be conscious of the interactions our children might be missing out on because of technoference. Have a think about your behaviour in the evening, when your child has come back from school and wants some of your attention but you're tired out from work. How easily distracted are you by your phone? How many times does your child say 'Mummy' or 'Daddy', and you're looking at your smartphone and say, 'In a minute!' I know this can happen to me more times than I feel comfortable with. When we're a bit exhausted, our smartphones can distract us more easily because our brain power is down and our potential for distractibility is higher. If you carry your phone around with you in the evenings, it's likely it will steal your attention away from your children, even when you don't really want it to. Diving into the digital world is a simpler, less emotive form of interaction than connecting with your children's physical and emotional needs.

At a basic level we all want to feel safe, seen and soothed, and this is ingrained in all of us from the very start of our lives. Your child is observing the world around them and noticing when your attention is on them rather than on other things. If you prioritise the alerts on your smartphone over the attempts at connection from your child, they'll get the message that smartphones have greater value, that whatever happens inside your smartphone must be more interesting, important and wanted than they are. When you allow technoference to happen, your actions will speak louder than your words. And at the end of the day, it is how your children experience being loved by you that matters, not your intentions to love them well.

Social skills are not innate; they're learnt in interaction with others. Teaching healthy communication begins with us; the behaviours we choose form deep connections with our children. For now, I want you to understand that our children feel most 'seen' by us when we're giving them our full attention and not putting our smartphones first. And after all, when looking back, I don't think anyone will have phubbing nostalgia, particularly when it comes to being with our children. It's highly unlikely that we'll ever bemoan the fact that we didn't spend more time on our phones. In Part Two, we'll come on to how our own smartphone use influences children's desire for these devices and how we can best model healthy smartphone habits to them.

Sharenting, and why you should be mindful of it

'Sharenting' is the pop-psychology term for the act of posting photos and videos of children online.

A national poll in 2015 of parents of children under the age of five in the United States found that:

- 56 per cent of mothers compared with only 34 per cent of fathers discussed personal information about their children on social media.
- 51 per cent revealed their child's location, such as their school or home address.
- 27 per cent shared photos and videos showing their child's face and body, dressed or undressed, sometimes in bathing suits or in the bath.[5]

Most parents do this with the intention of connecting with friends and family, to share proud moments or even help others feel less alone. I understand why parents do this, as I myself have done it too, but there are a lot of grey areas regarding a child's privacy, autonomy, protection and right to consent when we share information about them online. The information you share online might seem harmless, but when considered all together it can paint a picture of your child's life that can delay or disrupt the process of them growing their unique identities.

When a child's identity has begun online through their parents' view of them, it puts a representation of who they are into the world, which can impose an inadvertent pressure on a child to fit in with their projected online identity. Sharenting complicates children's sense of feeling seen, as you might unintentionally share parts of them that they don't want to show the world. Children need to be seen for who they are, not who you want them to be. When children become aware of sharenting it can lead to greater secrecy on their part, as they may withhold information for fear you will broadcast it to others. This can rupture the relationship of trust you've developed with them.

Sharing personal or potentially embarrassing information or photos for adult laughs can damage a child's self-esteem and lead to bullying in later years. Sadly, there are also more dangerous risks of sharenting. Any image that discloses personal information about your child (such as the first day at school photo with their uniform on), or an image where there's physical nudity, opens a window directly into your child's life that predators can exploit. It's easy to find out a child's age, school and home address, and you've probably already inadvertently shared their name. This information can lead to identity theft, exploitation, harassment . . . and worse. A recent report showed that bad actors and predators are using image generators with artificial intelligence (AI) to create sexually explicit content featuring children and teenagers (aka images of sexual abuse). Most of them are on the dark web, but some are on sites that are readily accessible. The source material for 90 per cent of the photos was reported to be images of fully clothed children whose faces were clearly visible, all posted on social media.

I most definitely have fallen into the trap of sharing photos of my children online with friends and family, and once I understood how it might impact my children growing up and the potential dangers of this, I removed the photos and stopped doing it. The reality is that once you put a photo online, it never disappears for good as it leaves a permanent digital footprint. Although I sometimes share photos of my children on my professional web page, it's always from behind, and I always show and ask my eldest for consent to share (for example, as a cover photo on my social media). If she doesn't like it or doesn't want to, I won't post. I'm aware that her understanding of the digital footprint is underdeveloped, so I always ask myself: 'Would I be upset if someone else was using this image?' If the answer is yes, I don't share it.

We've made it clear with family and friends that we don't want photos of our children online on any social media platform. This has been a tricky boundary for some extended family members, as they feel we've 'deprived' them of sharing photos in the same way their friends do online. It has at times created conflict and difficult conversations, including our message that we won't share any digital images of our children with members of our family who refuse to respect this boundary. We're choosing to value our children's identities and right to consent over adults' whims and wishes to imitate their friends' online behaviour.

If we model healthy smartphone behaviours and teach children that their digital privacy matters, we'll stand ourselves in better stead when we come to have the smartphone conversation with them when they're older.

> ### Reflect: is your online posting sharenting or safe?
>
> Before you share a photo, video or story about your child, use the following questions to guide you:
>
> - What's the purpose of posting this content? Is it necessary?
> - Have I asked my child's consent for what I'm about to share?
> - Is my child old enough to understand the concept of a digital footprint? If they're too young, how might they feel if they saw this information online when they're older?
> - Have I removed all possible identifying information?
> - Could someone use this content in ways that might disturb or upset me?
> - Am I sharing any information that might be personal, embarrassing or inappropriate for a partner, future employer or stranger to know about my child?

Smartphones can steal our attention and time away from our children. They can make us distracted, inattentive and less sensitive to the subtle signs and communications our children give us about their emotional states, creative endeavours or need for closeness. Consequently, we 'see' our children less and unwittingly leave them feeling less connected to us and less worthy of our attention. Smartphones are tricksters that give us all a false sense of closeness with others. While we might be socially available at all times of day, connecting via text doesn't offer us the human essence we need to sustain meaningful relationships.

Feeling seen isn't just necessary for healthy child development, it's fundamental to our social and emotional well-being as humans. Feeling seen promotes trust and acceptance, and impacts on our sense of belonging, self-worth and overall happiness. It's a paradox that although smartphones have opened up the digital world at our fingertips, they've inadvertently made us feel more alone and less connected to those around us. We must make a conscious effort to unlearn some of the ways we use our phones to promote more meaningful connection and role-model the behaviours we want our children to adopt one day when they carry one in their pockets too.

3

Soothed

Being soothed is critical to child development. It's only when a child's nervous system is in a calm state that they can learn to regulate emotions and develop healthy coping strategies. Being soothed helps children to better cope with stress and adversity.

Play is not just for fun

Many adults still dismiss play as a 'frivolous' activity, one that's solely undertaken for pleasure. Unless it's 'educational', these people believe that play doesn't offer skills that are productive or useful. This is a huge misconception based on a lack of understanding of child development and learning. Play is a highly effective way for children to relax and feel soothed. It can provide a safe space in which they can explore and express emotions, process difficult events and experiences, and it offers them a break from daily stressors and worries. Play is the foundation for many core skills in childhood, including social, emotional, physical and cognitive abilities. Evidence shows that in the first eight years of life, children learn better through play than through any form of academic teaching, which is why UNICEF's advocacy brief called play an essential strategy for learning.[1]

As adults, we mostly show love with our words and our touch. For children and teenagers, it's your presence during play that brings them connection and closeness.

Role play, pretend play and structured game play that follows rules face to face with toys, objects and you are all essential for healthy development. Play is a powerful medium for communication, learning and the understanding of everyday experiences. When children are young, play can bring them comfort and safety. You might see children replaying words, actions and events they've experienced. I'll never forget the day I heard my daughter say to her dolly, 'You're allowed to be angry, but my answer is no.' Yikes!

Play is a medium through which children practise social skills, find emotional release and make sense of things that are confusing, scary or overwhelming. It's also through play that you can connect with your child in a much deeper way than by just using words, and this isn't just true for little ones. Teenagers have a need for unstructured play where they can release stress and tension, and find their creativity. From a young age, children enjoy games with rules – and they frequently invent their own. These may include physical games such as chasing, hide and seek, and throwing and catching games, and, as children grow and mature, games such as board and card games, computer games and the whole variety of formal and informal sporting activities. Playing games is essentially social in nature and teaches children a range of skills, including sharing, taking turns, understanding others' perspectives and developing emotional regulation for those big, exciting wins and deeply upsetting losses.[2]

Playing games on smartphones isn't something that well-intentioned parents necessarily want to introduce to their children, but digital games done right can enrich play for children and their families, and can be done via tablets, laptops and video consoles.[3] I know some parents are concerned about the violence embedded into some video games, as well as the games' addictive nature. It's reassuring to know that well-designed computer games that offer open-ended or problem-solving challenges share some of the benefits of problem-solving or construction play with objects.[4] A global study by UNICEF looking at video games and children's well-being reported that there are two essential ingredients digital games must have to support well-being for six- to twelve-year-olds:

1. They represent and support equitable play for diverse children and childhoods.
2. They are, and feel, safe and secure.[5]

Put another way, they recommend that digital games should be accessible to all children in a way that emphasises the guiding principle of doing no harm. The research also highlighted the importance of families engaging in digital play experiences together to build on learning.

However, no single game can be all things to all children. In the same way that we wouldn't want a child to only play card games or only play with a ball, it's important to guard against children having excessive screen-based play, particularly when this is solitary and devoid of real-life interaction. We must focus on balance: indoor and outdoor, digital and real world, independent and social. The more diverse play experiences children have access to, the better the learning opportunities they'll have.

The UNICEF global study acknowledges that the digital games industry needs to work on reducing the risk of harm and invest in significantly more resources to keep children safe, especially on platforms where they're given the opportunity to socialise with others. Closed platforms, such as game consoles and payable apps such as Apple Arcade, ensure children are safe during digital play. When children start to play on a smartphone it's harder to control and understand exactly what they're playing and how safe it is. The responsibility of surveillance during digital play can feel harder and more overwhelming because it's time-consuming to make sense of all the games on offer, and the age ratings are often not reflective of a game's content. Moreover, even if a game has a low age rating, it might not be suitable for young children.

This is a similar situation to films, where a rating of PG doesn't necessarily mean it's an appropriate film for all children to watch. It means 'parental guidance' is advised, with the idea that you'll be watching it with your child and can choose to switch it off or walk away if it's found not to be appropriate. This might be the case with films, but how many parents sit alongside their children while they play video games and devote the time to understand what the content is showing?

Rather than thinking about online games as a vice, we need to reframe them as powerful tools that can offer our children enter-tainment, skills-building opportunities, and a chance to decom-press and self-soothe, when they play the right games in the right environment. We cannot forget to monitor our children during gameplay, however, just as we might monitor their ball games in the garden. And we must focus on memory-making play experiences, ensuring that children have time to experience play, fun, competition and all those critically important things that define growing up in real life too.

Frustration tolerance

We miss a real opportunity when we pull out our phones because we don't know what else to do. So many adults struggle with boredom, and if we can't tolerate it, it's going to prove impossible to teach our children to do so. But boredom is the crucible of curiosity, creativity and innovation; it not only gives you the space but also the discomfort that makes you want to fill that space with something else. For children to develop the skills that will lead them to feel soothed at times when they experience the discomfort of such emotions as frustration or boredom, they need to experience these and learn how to move through them. As that well-known children's book says: 'We can't go over it. We can't go under it. Oh no! We've got to go through it!'[6]

As a mother, I'm concerned about how seamlessly smartphones have become devices that offer an endless possibility of distractions. Life is not meant to be pleasurable every minute of the day, but with a smartphone you can curate a life where normal and healthy emotions such as boredom, sadness, frustration and anxiety all melt magically away. Unlike other types of screens, smartphones are carried on our person at all times, so it's impossibly easy to distract yourself away from something that brings discomfort to us or our children.

Recently we went out for pizza and sat opposite another family. They had two children, both on smartphones, the elder child around eleven and the younger a little older than my eldest, my guess was around seven or eight. As we ordered our food and then waited for far longer than expected, my eldest got fidgety. I'd forgotten to bring the activity books I usually pack for her, and when her little sister dropped some of the cutlery she'd been playing with onto the floor, she started to moan, 'I'm hungry!'. As a solution, we got her sister out of the high chair and they walked hand in hand, escorted by my husband, around the smallish restaurant, with our little one waving and squealing 'Hiya!' at every table. This was super-cute in my eyes, and movement is a great way to regulate their bodies and shake the boredom off, but I've no doubt it was probably deeply annoying to many of the other guests.

Later that evening my eldest brought up the subject of the other children at the restaurant. 'Why did they have their phones at the table?' she asked. Rather than superimpose my adult views onto her experience, I asked her, 'Why do *you* think?' She initially shrugged, then tentatively asked if maybe they were playing a fun game while they waited for their food. We talked about what she thought of this, what might be good about it, what she reckoned they might have missed out on and how it felt for her to see other children with smartphones at a restaurant. Our eldest knows she won't be getting a smartphone any time soon, and she's never used a screen at mealtimes. Now that she's a bit older, she's noticing that other families do things differently from us, and I know at some point that this is going to lead her to want things to be different for her too. For now, when these things crop up, we talk, I listen to her and we think aloud together. In her own words, 'If we were all on our smartphones we wouldn't get to chat or even see our food properly.' Well, exactly.

For me it's a no-brainer – enjoying quality family time together is not always easy, but mealtimes are a daily moment we can share simply by saying 'no' to smartphones. And on those rare occasions when we do go out, we keep it this way too. It doesn't necessarily make for a 'nice meal out' all the time, as it's often much more functional than that when our children accompany us. It's quick, it's as stress-free as possible, and as adults we enjoy it because we don't have to cook or wash up afterwards, which is a win–win for us. This is not to judge the parents in the restaurant, however. I think parents are in a real Catch-22: don't offer your child a smartphone, and you'll experience the gaze of judgement as your child speaks at the top of their voice, drops their cutlery or gets up and down too many times to satisfy social etiquette. But offer them a smartphone or a digital device so they stay seated quietly during the meal, and you'll get judged for that too. The truth is that parents are usually doing the best they can with what they have.

Knowing how to wait well is a life skill that many adults don't have. Why else do people get so enraged in a traffic jam, beeping their horns and shouting out of the window when no one is to blame and everyone is stuck? So many adults lack the skills to cope with frustration and boredom, and now that we all have smartphones in our pockets, is it even a necessary skill to develop? I'd argue that it's essential if we want our children to be able to find the necessary soothing and rest that are antidotes to our busy lives. This requires effort and means that you have to make a commitment to regulate your emotions so you can tolerate your children's feelings in those moments that test your patience. Children who possess little capacity to sit and wait for things often have difficulty tolerating frustration, disappointment or boredom, and they may struggle later in life as adults during moments that cannot get 'fixed' by a smartphone. These might include the frustration of having to wait until the end of the month to get paid and not being able to afford something you want, the disappointment of not getting a pay rise despite your hard work, the impatience that can accompany finding a home you can afford or even the wait to become a parent, which so often comes neither at the time nor in the manner we'd always hoped.

So much of adult life is about delayed gratification. Smartphones can give us the illusion of bypassing this by blocking feelings of discomfort and replacing them with endless possibilities for distraction. In the short term this might feel good or even appear to be soothing. But using smartphones in this way is an artificial plug that derails the development of healthy coping strategies for mature emotional development. As hard as it may be to accept, it's the choices we make that teach our children how to cope through the discomfort of the world.

Reflect: how are you teaching your child to cope with uncomfortable feelings?

Grab a notepad and answer the questions below, alone or as a parenting couple if you have a partner.

- What social opportunities does my child have to practise social and emotional skills?
- How do I support my child when they feel excited/ disappointed/frustrated during board games and other forms of entertainment with me and their friends?
- When do I allow my child to experience boredom without trying to fix or stop it?
- What situations or events lead me to experience frustration, boredom and discomfort? Can I use these moments as opportunities to model healthy coping strategies? List some actions of what you'll try to do.
- When does using a smartphone interfere with emotional-skills building or become a buffer for boredom and frustration?

In answering these questions, what have I learnt about myself and the things I need to learn and do so I can be a better guide for my child?

The hot topic of sleep

Studies consistently show that a large majority of teenagers, often exceeding 70 per cent, do not get the recommended nine to eleven hours of sleep a night that they need.[7] A number of interacting biopsychosocial factors affect teen sleep, and smartphones may compound this effect further.

Media headlines might tell you that 'blue light' emitted from smartphones is the main culprit behind bad sleep. These are based on a number of studies reporting that 'blue light' delays the natural production of the sleep hormone melatonin in the evening. The studies claim that children are particularly vulnerable to blue light and that they struggle to fall asleep when smartphones are around. Everyday household lighting, however, has also been found to affect melatonin production at night, with bright bedroom lights decreasing its production and delaying sleep by as much as ninety minutes compared with dim lighting, even if you're choosing to read a book rather than look at a screen.[8] Some studies have even looked at 'Night Shift', a mode that you can activate on an Apple iPhone that blocks blue light, but switching on 'Night Mode' doesn't impact on melatonin suppression (i.e. falling asleep later) or sleep quality.[9]

Even though blue light might not be to blame, it doesn't mean that smartphones have no impact on sleep. Some studies suggest smartphone use before bed can lead to greater alertness. A global review of twenty studies of more than 125,000 children aged between six and nineteen (with an average age of fifteen) showed that using a smartphone ninety minutes before going to bed could double the risk of disrupted sleep compared with the sleep of those in the same age range who didn't own a smartphone. Children who had a smartphone in their bedroom but didn't use it before bedtime were also found to experience poor sleep.[10] Other studies have found that children using a smartphone in their bedrooms were 31 per cent more likely to get less sleep than those who didn't, and the likelihood of poor sleep increased by 147 per cent when children engaged with a smartphone in the dark.[11] We therefore cannot consider smartphones' impact on sleep purely in the context of light emissions, we have to look at the effect of what we do online just before we go to bed.

There's a well-reported phase shift that occurs in the circadian rhythm of adolescents. Sleep pressure tends to build more slowly, which makes it easier for them to stay awake later at night.[12] It's possible that this biological shift, coupled with the 'always switched-on' nature of smartphones, means that children's minds are always engaged with devices in their environment, even when they're not actively using them. Smartphones are thought to affect sleep through a variety of ways, including delaying or interrupting sleep time, psychologically stimulating the brain and affecting natural sleep cycles. A TV show or film might come to a natural end that forces you to turn it off (eventually), but with a smartphone there's an endless flow of content that might capture your interest and keep your brain alert for longer, bypassing your natural body clock. This appears to have a greater impact when it happens in bedrooms and with the light switched off.

Sleep is an often undervalued but essential part of children's development. Sleep affects behaviour, irritability, performance and the ability to learn. During childhood, sleep is essential to enable developing brains to consolidate learning, recharge and feel soothed, so they can be at their best the following day. Although sleep recommendations by age tend to vary and individual sleep needs don't necessarily fit neatly into an hourly schedule, a rough guide by age is:

- four to twelve months: twelve to sixteen hours per day
- one to two years: eleven to fourteen hours per day
- three to five years: ten to twelve hours per night
- six to twelve years: nine to twelve hours per night
- thirteen to eighteen years: eight to thirteen hours per night[13]

There's lots you can do to promote positive sleep habits in the daytime and before bed. We'll explore these more in Part Two of this book (see page 212).

> ### Reflect: how do smartphones impact on sleep hygiene in your home?
>
> Take a moment to think about how smartphones might be having an impact on your sleep by focusing on your behaviour during the day:
>
> - How often do smartphones interrupt family mealtimes?
> - How does using a smartphone interfere or support your physical movement and that of your children? (Think: if you didn't have a smartphone, would you and your child move more or less than you do now?)
> - How many smartphones are kept in bedrooms? Knowing that even if you don't interact with it, a smartphone can lead to poor sleep simply by being in a bedroom, whose sleep is most impacted?

My smartphone recommendations

As a parent, nothing feels more crucial than making the right decisions on behalf of our children, and the responsibility of making these choices is permanently at the front of my mind. Because we're at the service of our children forever when we become parents, this is both a gift and weighty task. When it comes to modern parenting, smartphones are our greatest challenge. We're the first generation of parents to have to set the standard for what is 'right' during childhood in terms of access to the digital world.

We might say that owning a smartphone is only worthwhile if it makes our children better connected, safer, healthier human beings. I'm unsure, having reviewed the literature, whether smartphones have indeed made adults better connected, safer or healthier. But I also see and know that there's potential for all of us to do better. In this chapter, I've tried to offer you a balanced and evidence-based view of the risks and benefits of smartphones – both for us and for our children. In my view, while smartphones offer opportunities, none of these outweigh the risks of letting children with developing brains and growing hearts access the bottomless pit of harmful content and overwhelming sensory stimulation that comes with having a smartphone. *Unless the potential benefits outweigh the harms, we should be delaying children from accessing smartphones for as long as is possible.*

Social media was never created for children, but the tech companies have sussed out that there is a market for children and they're extracting business from them and us, their parents. Even so, most social media apps have a minimum age to access them of thirteen, including Instagram, Facebook, Snapchat, X and Reddit. In the European Union they advise that children must be sixteen years old before accessing WhatsApp or Tumblr. And yet, we know by the age of eleven smartphones are ubiquitous and many children access social media platforms and messaging apps, with or without parental consent. It's just too tempting not to! We can all be doing better by not being blind to the potential harms smartphones offer children and simply say 'no', delaying giving them smartphones until they're closer in age to what the tech companies themselves are setting as age limits.

As a clinical psychologist, and given the evidence I've outlined in this first part of the book, I believe children shouldn't own a smartphone before the age of thirteen. In our family, and as parents to two daughters, we're aiming for fifteen. Even if our time points are different, the good news is that you've got the parental authority to decide when your child should have the responsibility of carrying a smartphone, and if you start out with calm confidence, and clear rules and expectations, it can make delaying a lot easier.

When I think about it now, what I'll say to my daughters might sound something like this:

I need to teach you which parts of having a smartphone are safe, useful and necessary, and which parts to avoid. If there's a part that's new to me or you, then we need to be cautious about how we explore it, and do it together. You need to learn to not stay on a smartphone for too long or go in too deep. When you can learn the signals from your body and know how to follow safe steps, smartphones can be wonderful tools that can be fun too. But learning these skills takes time, practice and lots of support. A bit like swimming in the sea, you need to stay close to the shore and learn how to swim confidently before you can venture further out. That's why I won't be getting you your own smartphone until you're fifteen, and I know the wait is going to feel really hard.

No one showed me how to use a smartphone safely, what the dangers of going in too deep were or how to get out when I'd been using one for too long. Many adults like me jumped straight into the smartphone sea and shot off into deep water without ever learning how to swim first. Now we know more, we can do better, and what I've learnt I can pass on to you. This means that you won't make the same mistakes I made, and you'll never have to feel like you're out of your depth or at risk of drowning. The day you get a smartphone, I want you to feel like you know what you're doing, that you can do it well, and that the mini supercomputer in your pocket is a wonderful tool that will help you and bring you fun and joy at times too. I promise to help you get there, and we can talk about this as often as you need to.'

I don't know if I'll ever read this to them out loud just as I've written it here, or whether I'll have learnt the essence of it by heart given the many times I've turned it round and round in my head. What I do know is that writing it down has helped me think about my 'why' and given me greater confidence in my decision. It's created a story that empowers me to stay grounded in my parenting authority to make this choice for my children. Delaying a smartphone until they're fifteen (or as near as possible to this age) is something I feel I need to do to have the time to teach my children how to use one safely without them acquiring the same bad habits that I've got. For this to happen, I have to commit to working on my relationship with my smartphone and become a better role model. I know I'll make reams of mistakes, but my hope is that rather than crumbling under the weight of this responsibility, I can use my mishaps as opportunities to teach important lessons to my children before they ever have the opportunity of making the same ones. The second part of this book, the Family Phone Pledge Plan, will walk you through how to implement a delay and make it a success.

I know tech companies have a responsibility too, but the duty of care for our children's well-being lies primarily with us. It's the important job we signed up for the day we became parents. I take my responsibility very seriously, as I know you do too (why else would you have got this far into the book?). I want you to know that it's never too late. If you have an older child who has a smartphone, the ship has not yet sailed. It's still in the harbour and there's plenty of room to slow it down sufficiently to stop it from advancing into the choppy seas without your child having a life-jacket on. You can protect your children from the impact of smartphones, and your best tool for this is *you*.

If there's one recurring theme from the smartphone conversation, it's the need to build strong foundations of connection and trust with our children so we can set tight boundaries that protect them. You cannot have one without the other. Before smartphones are even a 'thing' in your child's life, you need to focus on your relationship with them. Children need hands-on physical, emotional and social connection. We need to play with our children and make this time important. We need to learn to put our phones away so we can be present when it matters and show our children we value them more than the digital world we carry in our phones. We need to model the behaviour we want them to effortlessly practise when they gain access to a smartphone because they've experienced what good, healthy habits looked like from day one in their homes – we'll cover this in more detail next.

Connection is the antidote to smartphones. It acts as a buffer to external pressure. When we're closely connected to our children, they're less likely to lose themselves when they go online. Because when they feel seen, safe and soothed in the real world and in their relationship to us, they don't need to seek these basic needs online. So even when they engage online, they're less likely to lose themselves completely.

It's clear that research is still needed in many areas to understand the impact of smartphones, but waiting for this research to be carried out is not an option. Given the science we have, it's hard to see how the benefits of using a device that has unfiltered access to the internet outweigh the risks inherent in social media and the possibility of finding content that's distressing, sexualised, inappropriate and with the potential to harm. Delaying smartphones in childhood is just smart, healthy common sense.

Takeaways

There's solid research showing that 'screen time' isn't a concern in itself and that using screens for academic pursuits is helpful. But screens are still a potential distraction to real-world experiences, and we must focus on the balance between online and offline engagement, as well as the content our children are viewing.

The idea that screens and smartphones are addictive is false, but a helpful reframing is to think about the bad we have created with digital technologies. How we live with our smartphones is the greatest influence on how our children live with theirs in the future.

Social media was not created for children. It offers content to children that's distressing and has the potential to harm young minds and young hearts in ways they're unable to cope with. Social media places those who are most vulnerable – such as children who already suffer from anxiety and low mood, or who are targets of bullying from their peers – at greater risk, as their vulnerabilities are amplified online. Being aware of who your child is and their mental health risks is an absolutely vital consideration in this respect.

Smartphones offer the illusion of safety but can place children at physical risk as targets of theft, and using tracking software can rupture the delicate relationship of trust that has developed between children and parents.

Meaningful social contact is important and smartphones can give us access to this when we use them well. But when all we do is send texts and online messages, we lose the human essence that brings us connection. So rather than feeling more closely connected to others, we risk suffering from loneliness.

You can have too much of a good thing. Online socialising can become overwhelming and anxiety-provoking, with its potential influx of relentless messages. Children have a need to socialise, but smartphones can turn this into a stressor rather than an opportunity.

Digital play has been shown to be beneficial and to complement real-world play, as long as there's a balance and you're choosing closed platforms that keep your child safe. Mostly this can happen away from a smartphone by choosing video consoles, tablets and laptops.

Smartphones can be a fun diversion, but they can also be unhelpful if they're constantly used to block uncomfortable emotions such as boredom, frustration and impatience.

'Technoference' is the way in which smartphones rupture face-to-face social interaction. All of us would do well to watch out for this and set better social boundaries to avoid sending our children the message that what we do online is of greater value than being present with them. We should become aware of how technoference impacts on the relationships we have with our children, and how it diverts our attention away from them, erecting barriers that inhibit the art of conversation with those we cherish. We should equally stop ourselves from 'phubbing' others and model more appropriate social behaviour, the same sort that we're so keen to teach our children.

Sleep is often overlooked as an essential need for children. We must support better sleep and rest, and when screens are used for soothing and relaxation, we should focus on the content children are watching and limit smartphone use in bedrooms. Smartphones should not be the 'go-to' device at bedtime, and we should protect our sleep and that of our children by creating good sleep hygiene routines in our homes.

My recommendation is that parents delay smartphones for their children until they are at least thirteen. While you delay, help your children learn how to use technology well through active teaching and role-modelling the behaviours you want to see more of.

Part Two

The Family Phone Plan

Delaying smartphones is no small feat as it takes courage for parents to say 'not yet' and go against the norm. If you feel overwhelmed by the prospect of doing this, worry that your child will feel left out or that you will be judged by other parents, fear not. I've created the Family Phone Plan for you.

In this second part of the book, I'll offer you seven evidence-based steps to develop your own family 'road map' for when it comes to delaying smartphones:

1. **It starts with you** – Looking at your relationship and habits with your smartphone, giving you a chance to sense check how healthy they are and what you can put in place to change them if they need tweaking, and considering your parenting style and the best ways to find your confident parenting authority.
2. **Understanding your child** – Making sense of the 'phone flags' that you might witness and how to support your child through them, and what the best fit between your child's

unique temperament and their interaction with the online world might look like.

3. **Open and honest dialogue** – The best way to say 'not yet' and help you see the art of waiting for a smartphone as a positive opportunity for your family.

4. **Join the Family Phone Pledge** – A promise I invite you to make as a family to delay smartphones and work together as a team to make this stick. It's also an opportunity to extend it forward to friends and family in your community so you can network, reap maximum support and problem-solve when challenges occur. We are not supposed to navigate the challenge of smartphones alone – there is power in doing this together.

5. **Involving others** – Scripts, letters and ideas to help you communicate your smartphone boundaries and expectations to others around you, how to bring older siblings into the fold and act as positive role models, and some thoughts on the supportive and safe role schools might play to join us in this.

6. **Find your SPARK** – Strategies and toolkits to help you make the Family Phone Pledge stick in ways that are simple and actionable. I have broken this down into sections that look at how you **s**ocialise, stay **p**resent, **a**ccess online worlds, protect **r**est and sleep, and develop your **k**nowledge about smartphones and digital media. Rather than feel overwhelmed, this should help you feel equipped to make small adaptations that have long-term impact.

7. **Digital resilience** – Tools to help you teach your child skills to stay safe online when they get access to a smartphone.

Because protecting our children is good, but preparing them alongside protection is better.

I believe in our individual power to create societal change. As parents, we can revolutionise what the norm with smartphones is.

Step 1

It starts with you

Picture the scene. Your child has been watching reruns of *Gladiators* for an hour while you prepare dinner. You feel they've watched enough, so you shout down the hall, 'Switch that off!' Later that evening, your child is telling you a story about the Beyblade challenge that took place at school when your WhatsApp alert chimes. You pick up your smartphone and, while your child is still talking, you begin to respond to the message. Whether you intend to or not, your behaviour is telling your child: 'Screens are not good for you when you're a child, but when you become a grown-up they become more valuable than the people around you.'

I believe that delaying smartphones is the right choice, but if we're to implement a delay effectively, we need to model the importance of building genuine relationships and connections through face-to-face interactions, stress the value of spending time with friends and family, and participate in activities with our children that foster meaningful connections, experiences and memories. It's how we live with our screens and smartphones, not how we tell our children to live, that will help them understand our decision to delay their possession of a smartphone and offer them a template for sensible smartphone habits in the future.

This chapter helps you to consider how delaying smartphones might feel for you, and the rules that are going to make most sense for you and your child in your home. We will start with thinking about your relationship with smartphones and screens.

Your parenting practices

The strongest influence on your parenting is how you were parented as a child. For many years, you had a front-row seat to 'parenting' that will have made an indelible impression on you. Your parents' and carers' words and actions while they parented you form a foundation from which many of the decisions you make with your children stem.

Sometimes your parents provided an example of what to do that you will imitate, and at times their behaviour might serve as an example of what not to do, leading you to make different parenting decisions with your children. The tricky bit is this: if you weren't born in the smartphone age, your parents never made any decisions, good or bad, about what was 'right' for you in terms of smartphones, leaving you with no model to guide your decisions right now.

Our parenting practices also align with the culture and values of the society we live in. What is and isn't acceptable around us influences some of the decisions we make. For example, no parent in Western society today would drive off in a motor vehicle without first ensuring their child was fastened in by a seatbelt. In our parents' generation, however, driving without a seatbelt on was widely practised, and no one would have done a double-take seeing a child sitting in the boot of an estate. When it comes to smartphones, our society has not yet got to grips with what's 'safe' or 'healthy', and there are no regulations around smartphone ownership for children. It therefore falls on us, as parents, to establish rules about what 'safe' and 'healthy' look like.

Parenting isn't a one-size-fits-all exercise. Your parenting style and personality influence the choices you make around your child and the confidence with which you'll find your 'no'. If you tend to be more anxious and risk-averse, you're more likely to be protective of your child and might find saying 'no' to smartphones comes more easily. If you struggle setting limits and boundaries, however, you might try to avoid conflict and be more likely to go with the flow of what those around you are doing. So, when your children's friends get a smartphone, it might feel tricky to stand out as the only one who says 'no'. As much as we might all like to believe that our parenting decisions are based solely around our children's needs, it's our personalities, our experiences, and the thoughts and feelings we have about smartphones that shape our decisions and the confidence with which we make them.

Children tend to respond better to rules when they think their parents are being fair and reasonable. In 2019 a thousand teenagers were presented with scenarios where parents were trying to set boundaries on technology by using threats and punishment to enforce the rules (authoritarian), or guiding them in a supportive way, listening and valuing their opinions, and explaining the reasons for the boundary or limit (authoritative). Teenagers were asked how they would react in each situation, and if you know anything about parenting styles it might not surprise you to hear that the teenagers facing the authoritarian and more punitive approaches said they were more likely to break the rules and more inclined to go behind their parents' back when using smartphones.

The teens who were presented with more supportive scenarios said that while they'd also try to rebel against the rules (because, let's be honest, that's just a rite of passage for teenagers), they'd be less inclined to hide their use of technology from their parents and would be more likely to go to them if something went wrong. Teenagers are going to rebel against the rules we set them; it's part and parcel of adolescence. But it's only when we know what our children are up to that we can support and keep them safe. How you choose to talk about smartphones and set the rules around them is deeply important, and one of the reasons why outright bans can have long-term negative effects.

Have a look at the following breakdown of parenting styles. We all fall into more than one category depending on the context (for example, you might notice yourself being more permissive on holiday but become authoritarian when you've repeated the same instruction for the twentieth time). Overall, we want to work towards being authoritative most of the time because this is the parenting style that has been shown to have the most positive outcomes (more about why this matters in relation to our children and smartphones later). Take a moment to reflect on these parenting styles and the things you might like to try doing differently. You can come back to refer to this table whenever you need a reminder.

Parenting style	Benefits and challenges	What you could do differently
Authoritative 'I am here for you. Let's talk.'	You set clear rules and expectations around smartphone use. You consider your child's age, maturity level and ability to cope with risk before getting them a smartphone. You understand the need for communication, and you listen to your child's views and consider them. You set the right environmental safeguards for your child to access the digital world safely, such as limiting screen time, monitoring online activities and having open conversations about online content. You're present and active around your child when they go online until they're developmentally old enough and skilled enough to navigate it independently.	If you're doing this most of the time, you're doing amazingly well!
Authoritarian 'My house, my rules!'	You might be more likely to impose outright bans on smartphones. You might minimise or dismiss your child's experiences or wishes. You might prioritise obedience and compliance over your child's need for independence.	Listen to your child with a view to understanding them better. Support them to have safe online experiences with you by their side.

(Continued)

(*Continued*)

Permissive 'I trust you to be OK.'	You might be lax on boundaries to avoid confrontation. You might struggle to set clear limits because you don't know how to stand your ground. You might monitor your child's online activities less, believing your child has a right to autonomy and can make their own choices.	Set clear family rules around screen time. Spend time talking about your child's online world to understand their experiences. Learn to tolerate your child's anger and get comfortable with being in charge.
Uninvolved 'I don't have time for this. You do you.'	You might have a sense that the online world is mostly safe. You might be indifferent to or unaware of what your child does online. You might have no time to supervise or monitor your child's online activity. Your child might have more 'online freedom' than others, placing them at greater potential risk.	Use age-appropriate parenting controls to safeguard your child. Open up a dialogue about screen time and digital experiences. You may benefit from asking for help from a professional to support you in finding your confident parental authority.

Your parenting style is likely to influence how you introduce smartphones to your child, and the rules and expectations that you deem necessary when you do so. If you want to work at becoming more authoritative, consider what steps you need to do this:

If you tend towards being authoritarian, consider building a closer relationship with your child. Spend time together, listen to their views and empathise with the things that matter to them.

If you lean towards being permissive, reflect on why finding your parenting authority feels hard. Are you worried that boundaries might make you harsh or punitive? Learn to set firm boundaries with love. This looks like: empathise with your child + set the boundary + express warmth towards them. For example: 'I know you want a smartphone like your friends have' (empathy) + 'You can have one when you turn thirteen, but not yet' + 'I hate seeing you sad but it's my job to keep you safe. You're allowed to be angry with me.'

If you feel like you might be closer to being uninvolved, it's likely your time is overstretched and there might be work, life or family pressures that make it difficult for you to be as present and available to your child as much as you'd like. Try to use parenting controls to help you set a layer of protection and make intentional choices about the devices your child uses and the content they have access to when these are available to them.

How do you use your smartphone?

Children learn more by what you do than what you say. We have good evidence to show that if we want to help our children learn healthy digital habits, we need to lead by example. How you feel and behave with your phone is crucial in shaping your child's attitudes to smartphones. If you limit your child's screen time but don't monitor your own, or set rules in your home for when phones get switched off but ensure they don't apply to you, it will send your child mixed messages and make it more likely that you'll end up fighting daily battles about why it's OK for you to have a phone at the dinner table but not them. Since birth, children have seen adults use phones and, over time, they're learning what is and isn't acceptable. Modelling healthy phone use and encouraging our children to be part of this, including pointing out when we overuse our phones, allows children to get on board with our family rules, rather than push against them.

Before we broach the issue of smartphones with our children, we need to examine our own relationship with smartphones – the ones we carry in our pockets – and consider how we lead by example. The 'smartphone health check' questionnaire below has been adapted from a few questionnaires concerning smartphone use. This is not a diagnostic tool, but it's helpful to see how we use our phones laid out in black and white. Try to do this with an open mind and be kind to yourself – if you don't like what you see, I'm going to give you the tools to change things.

We often don't see our behaviour the way others experience it. If you feel courageous enough, do this questionnaire with someone who has experience of the relationship you have with your phone. If you're an adult, ideally that would be your partner, but it might also be an extended family member with whom you spend lots of time, or a close friend.

See this as a way to reflect on your smartphone and screen use and the impact it has in your home, which we will dive into deeper next.

Smartphone health check for adults

Do you check your phone too much?

A. My phone checking gets in the way of things I need to do. Sometimes I lose hours scrolling and forget I was doing work or a domestic task.

B. I check it when I need to but it doesn't distract me from what I'm doing.

C. I don't check it very often. I miss messages from work/ friends all the time.

What's the first thing you reach for when you wake up?

A. My phone – it's my alarm clock.

B. My phone – I need to check emails/messages.

C. A cuddle with my partner/child.

When you need to check the time, where do you look?

A. On my phone.

B. On my laptop.

C. My watch/clock.

How often do you take photos/videos on your phone?

A. Every day.

B. Only when something special is happening, such as a birthday or a significant event.

C. Never. I carry a camera when I need to take photos.

How likely are you to use your phone somewhere you shouldn't, such as while driving, at the cinema or in a work meeting?

A. Very likely if it buzzes. I want to know what the notification is.

B. Sometimes when it's really necessary, such as a call from school.

C. Not at all likely. I switch my phone off/put my phone away when I'm not supposed to use it.

How likely are you to text someone who's in the same room/house as you?

A. Very likely.

B. It's rare, and only if there's a reason why I cannot move or speak, such as when I need help but don't want everyone around me to know.

C. I'd never do this.

Where is your phone right now?

A. I'm using it to read this quiz!

B. It's beside me/on my person.

C. It's somewhere nearby but not on me.

Scoring: 2 points for A, 1 point for B, 0 points for C.

If you scored 10 points or more, ask yourself the important questions:

- Does realising you rely on your phone a lot bother you?
- Does it bother anyone else? Do you hear your partner or children ever say, 'Put the phone down'?
- Does your phone use ever get in the way of things you want to do, such as distracting you from your work so you miss deadlines? Does scrolling in bed stop you from falling asleep? Do you ever miss lunch because you've been taking a 'break' on your phone but not eaten a single bite?

The higher your score, the more you rely on your smartphone. Use this as a guide to see where some of the problem areas may be for you. For example, if you answered 'A – My phone' to 'What's the first thing you reach for when you wake up?', try buying an old-school alarm clock and put your phone in a different room, so when you wake up it's no longer the first thing you touch. What follows are some more ideas for changing your own behaviour around smartphones. You might also like to come back and reflect on your changes after a few weeks of embedding new strategies in your home.

Strategies for addressing your smartphone usage

Childhood is fleeting. The first word they say, their first steps, how they look on their first day of school, their first Christmas recital, their first school disco . . . All these precious firsts don't come round again. Smartphones help us snap a moment to store in our capsule of memories, and it only takes seconds. They also let us celebrate and share moments with others who aren't with us physically but can join us in virtual joys in the blink of an eye. But do we need to capture every moment through a lens? And is it necessary to continuously share online what we do in real life, for others to see too? Before we get on to thinking about our family smartphone habits, it's worth spending some time to make sure you feel good about yours.

Recently my daughters started playing together. They'll both be hanging around the toy kitchen making drinks and trays of wooden-shaped food in their 'café' to feed to their soft toys carefully lined up on the floor, and us, their parents. The little one toddles about carrying the trays, and they often crash and fall to the floor with a resounding, 'Uh oh!' Her elder sister comes to her rescue and reassures the 'customers' that 'It's all right, the food's OK. You can still eat it.' These mini role plays and interactions between them are moments of pure joy that I desperately want to capture on my phone. But the more I've started to reflect on my relationship with my phone, the more I've started to realise that not only does so much magic happen off camera that I don't need to capture to make it real, but also the more my children see me capturing what they're doing through my smartphone camera lens, the more likely they are to want to have one so they can do the same. Rather than making my children the lead characters of our family documentary, I want to join them in their real-life adventures. Because childhood is a 'time-limited series', and although we'd like to rewind and replay, we won't get to live these moments again.

That doesn't mean to say you can't ever capture special moments on camera. At my child's dance performance, I agreed with another parent to do the filming between us and share the footage so we could tuck our phones away and be present most of the time. This tiny tweak seems small but makes a big difference to the meaning you take from experiences. The shared physiological and empathetic response that has been called 'collective effervescence' comes from sharing our human experience with others, not through tangible and concrete things, but through human connection and interaction.

It's the knowing smile shared with another parent before a performance, the moment your child's eyes catch yours and their entire body lights up with the reassurance that their favourite person is in the audience. It's the moment you sit on the sofa side by side and see your child's quivering lip that tells you something is up, and without words you can open your arms and show them, 'Come here. What's up?' It's the long sigh from your child doing exam revision, and when you catch their gaze as you walk past, your smile tells them, 'I know it's hard. You're nearly there.' But with your eyes glued to a screen you miss these milliseconds of opportunity to connect with your child. They're the foundation of our shared human experience, where meaning and memories are made from a sense of being seen and understood by someone. And your child is always going to want that someone to be you.

Small consistent steps can turn into habits

You're going to be distracted by the many tasks you juggle as a parent, this is unavoidable. Work deadlines, household chores, the cooking, cleaning and evening routine, not to mention the alerts, buzzing and intrusions that come from your smartphone. Although your child doesn't need you to be present and engaged in all they do and say, you also don't want to send the message that what happens inside your phone is more important than what happens in their life. Trust me, there are more opportunities to put down your phone than you may think. You've got the ultimate control of the choices you make, and despite it possibly being unfamiliar and strange at first, you absolutely can stop to pause and reflect before you pick up your phone to answer a message, check your social media or even take a snapshot of a special moment. Sometimes, all of this can wait, and you can learn to set limits and do things differently. For example, by wearing a watch you might come to rely less on the clock on your phone, or deleting your email app might create a boundary for your work time and where you choose to read your emails. Doing these things doesn't have to be difficult or complicated, and it might help you feel more connected to your child and the world around you. It might make us all a little more human too.

Changing behaviour takes time, and the biggest mistake you can make is to think that doing it all at once is going to be more effective. It's the reason why so many people who get a gym membership in January cancel it after their three months' grace period or why a 'digital detox' doesn't last more than a week or two – it's just not sustainable.

I want you to be successful in the endeavour of embedding healthier habits with your phone and finding a toolkit that works for you. Before we go into what this might look like, you need to do two things:

- Start with a small change.
- Commit to keep going.

That's it. Choose something small and keep doing it. You're likely to mess up and forget about doing it every now and again, and that's just part of the process of embedding a new habit. And it's important to remember that your old habit won't disappear overnight. For example, you can keep checking your phone repeatedly or look at the screen every time it buzzes, but when you commit to creating new habits, old ones will become weaker and stop being your go-to behaviour. When you revert to an old habit, rather than giving up, just pick up your new small action once again. The day it becomes something you simply do rather than have to plan or think about, you'll know you've created a habit, and that's when you might choose to add another small change and another and another. Soon you'll have added enough new behaviours and tools that give you the sense that you're in a good place, enjoying a healthier, happier relationship with your smartphone, one you're proud of modelling to your children.

Two tips to become more intentional with your phone

If you want to become more intentional with your phone, using it when it matters and putting it out of the way when it doesn't – just like you'd pick up a wooden spoon to stir the pot rather than hold it in your hand the whole way through the cooking process – I've got two powerful ideas to help you.

Tip 1: use a visualisation

Visualisations help to embed habits because they prepare your brain by mentally rehearsing a desired behaviour. Our brain doesn't distinguish between real or imagined when you're creating or strengthening neural pathways. If you imagine yourself performing a behaviour, the same areas of your brain that would become active during the actual behaviour get stimulated, strengthening the neural connections linked with that action. Using visualisations can also build confidence when you're doing something new.

Try this: visualise that whenever you open your smartphone, you're unlocking a door into the digital world. Try to visualise your phone screen as a door and the passcode as the key. You can choose to open the door or to keep it shut.

When I am with others, this visualisation helps me to think more mindfully about whether I really need to open the door. Is it appropriate to do it right now? And if the answer is, 'Yes I need to, and it's appropriate,' I'll then ask myself: 'How will I communicate to those around me that I am temporarily "walking out" of the real world and opening the door to spend some time online?' In real life, this might sound like: 'I just need to check some of these messages, do you mind? I'll be back' and I can then take myself physically or metaphorically away. In truth, doing this has led me to 'open the door' into the digital world a lot less when I'm in the physical company of others. It has made me pause before choosing to 'turn the key'. The second thing I've noticed when doing this is that if I've opened the door to the digital world once, I'm less likely to do it again in the company of the same people, because staring at a screen intermittently is a bit like getting up and leaving to use the toilet every ten minutes . . . at some point, someone's going to ask if something's wrong.

Tip 2: use affirmations

This might sound a little 'woo woo', but hear me out. Reciting positive affirmations or having them written down in places you look at frequently and can see at regular times – such as on your bathroom mirror, on your fridge or on the back of your front door – will focus your attention, give you pause for thought and activate your prefrontal cortex, which helps with planning and organising. In other words, reciting positive affirmations will shift your brain into believing you *can* do a behaviour, and over time this will make the behaviour more likely to happen.

The trick with affirmations is that first, you need to use positive language (so avoid using 'don't', 'can't' and words like 'loss' that equate to scarcity) and second, they only truly work when the language is tailored to you. I will offer some ideas of what a good, positive affirmation looks like, but feel free to adapt them to make them work for you.

- 'I can let go of my phone.'
- 'I look around me when I walk down the street and see new things every day.'
- 'When I see friends, I love chatting to them and I put my phone in my bag.'
- 'When I spend time with my children, I put my phone on charge, and I enjoy being present.'
- 'I enjoy the lightness of not carrying my phone on my person.'

Affirmations are more powerful when you remind your brain you're doing something better than you were previously doing. And whenever old habits creep in, for example, 'I don't scroll on my phone in the evenings any more,' try and reframe this in ways that are congruent with the new world you're living in, not the old one you're leaving behind. This might sound like, 'I enjoy reading in the evenings' or 'I love catching up on the latest series and talking about it afterwards.'

Impatience flies in the face of new habits. Don't be upset if doing this seems hard at first. Visualisations and affirmations are not magic, they take practice and repetition. For some, they're a strange thing to do, which is why I invite you to write the visualis-ation and a few affirmations down on Post-it notes and leave them round the house. Any time you see one, read it two or three times in your mind. See how this lands. You could also write the visualisation out and take a photo of it as your screensaver. Next time you look at your phone it will remind you that you're about to use a key to open the door into the portal of the internet, which might help you make a more intentional choice.

We sometimes find it difficult to accept that what we do affects our children more than what we say. Looking at our own habits with smartphones can feel confronting, but rather than feel bad about it, I hope you can see it's a good opportunity to make tweaks towards having healthier habits, and you also get the honour of leading your child by example.

If you mess up, the best thing to do is to not give up. Stick to the changes you want to make and remind yourself of your 'why': to build healthier habits with smartphones that your children can learn from; to have a better balance between your offline life and the online worlds you choose to inhabit; to feel more connected to those you love and the world around you. Think about your reasons and remind yourself that these choices are important.

It's also useful to explain to your child what it is that you're doing. For example, explain how scrolling steals time from you that could be spent doing more important things, or how you've noticed you don't always pay them your full attention because your phone is highly distracting, so putting it on charge in a different room is helping you.

The way you choose to live with your smartphone is giving your child the biggest example of how they're going to live with phones in the future. Although the changes you're making are hard, you can keep working on them one step at a time. Don't give up. I am alongside you, doing this too.

Delaying doesn't mean 'no', it means 'not yet'

When you start adapting your behaviour to become a better role model around smartphones, you will start to build confidence in your parental authority to set limits and delay the acquisition of these devices. By doing it for yourself, you will gain experience of what might work well and where the struggles might show up. This will help you become more empathetic towards your child and the difficulty that they might find with waiting. Being more intentional with your time will also offer you the natural rewards and positive feelings that come from better sleep, more meaningful social interactions and greater connection as a family. These will help you and your children to keep these behaviours up.

I want you to think about delaying smartphones as an act of love that can be empowering to both you and your child. When we impose a ban on smartphones we instantly make them more desirable. Anything we cannot have inevitably becomes something we're more curious about and want to get our hands on. But when we say, 'not yet', we tell our children that smartphones are not out of bounds to them, they're simply not ready to have one with unimpeded access to all the apps and content they offer. 'Not yet' opens up a conversation. It tells children that we're not ignoring their wishes, and one day they will indeed get a smartphone, but there's learning to be done before that happens.

What's being presented to them is an opportunity to delay gratification, a key life skill that children need in order to develop resilience and self-regulation, and to feel gratitude. It focuses on what children need to do and learn, rather than on what they cannot have. Smartphones should not be dangled in front of children as bribes or treats to get them to behave in a certain way. Smartphones are not 'rewards' children get to access at some point in their lifetime. We need to see it in the same way that we look at cars – they're a luxury item with a specific purpose, and they require certain skills, knowledge and a big dose of responsibility, because using them carries physical risks to the driver and to those around them.

A hard 'no' can often feel like a rejection, but when you choose to delay smartphones you're offering your child the time and space to work at developing digital skills in the real world. These include having face-to-face relationships and growing social skills that will help them when they go online, learning emotional regulation and how to cope with big feelings, which will go a long way in protecting them from engaging in harmful communications online, learning when it's time to take a screen break, and building healthy habits around digital devices such as tablets, laptops and the TV. These habits will help them transfer the same boundaries to a smartphone, protecting everyday moments and relationships, not to mention their sleep, from becoming consumed by the digital world.

Importantly, delaying smartphones emphasises the fact that they're not a 'toy' to be used by children. Smartphones shouldn't be considered an object for fun, filters and games, a status symbol or rite of passage into secondary school. They're both a wonderful tool and a dangerous machine. We need to teach our children to use smartphones well, and that's going to take time. I see delaying smartphones as a gift to our children, to let them build skills we never had – and may still be working on – so they can incorporate smartphones into their lives in a better way than we've done so far. Technology is not inherently bad. Smartphones can be wonderful and help us stay connected with others, give us access to unlimited sources of information and bring us closer to other human beings. We can teach our children to use smartphones in a way that works *for* them, rather than against them, if we can just protect these early years of development to give them – and us – a chance to do so as best we can.

Setting boundaries

The one thing that helps children respect a boundary is having clear expectations from the get-go. It's important that these are established outside of any arguments or battles around screens or phones. In the same way in which we might have a conversation about driving and why children cannot get behind a steering wheel, we can have conversations that set the stage before they even ask about smartphones, and these will help them understand why they're not for children. Do this regularly in a conversational style that normalises the expectation of delaying a smartphone. It's not a big deal, it's just what it is.

Say it: 'Smartphones are not for children'

This is so simple, but how many parents have actually said it? Let your child know that smartphones are not things that children can use, manipulate or own. Instead, be present around them if or when they use your smartphone for any reason. For example, my eldest likes to take photos, and we've now bought her a little digital camera with which she loves taking photos of her toys and creating photographic memories of her play. She'll also occasionally use our smartphone when we're out and about, such as when we're on holiday, and when she does so we say loud and clear, 'You can take a photo like this and I'm trusting you to hold it very carefully. Smartphones are really expensive – they're not toys and they're not for children.' We never unlock our phone and we stay close by, supervising her while she's taking snaps. She enjoys sharing her images with us, which we keep in a folder, and she's allowed to look at them when we're beside her to supervise.

Make the age limit clear

You don't have to wait until your child asks, 'When can I get a phone?' to tell them, 'You won't be getting a phone until you're at least thirteen.' When children are young they don't need to fully understand why this is the case, but they do benefit from knowing that there's an age when you might start to consider a smartphone as an option for them. And if you say this, guess what happens? Most children get excited. They might start counting how many years there are for them to 'get' to thirteen. But because you've said, 'Not yet,' instead of, 'You're not getting a smartphone,' there's a lot of hope and possibility in those words that children will grab on to.

Discuss smartphones when you see them

Perhaps you're walking down the street and see a lot of people staring at their phones while going about their business. Point this out to your child, even though it may sound like, 'Gosh, there are so many people walking around, looking at their phones. It's amazing they don't trip over!' Or perhaps, after popping in to a café, you can talk about your child's reaction to seeing people sitting across from each other in silence and scrolling on their phones. Ask your child, 'What do you think they were doing?' and 'What do you think they might have been doing if they hadn't had their phones?' These two questions can lead to an interesting conversation. Try to avoid criticising other people as much as possible while emphasising that being on their smartphone didn't look like fun, something like, 'Hmm . . . maybe they were still working or finishing their online shopping . . . Sounds less fun than chatting with the other person across the table, that's for sure.'

You have parental power to say 'no'

Whether it's regarding a smartphone or an app, a game or a website, you can always say 'no', and when it comes to phones, that can stretch to a full sentence. Our eldest is only six and she knows our rules around smartphones. Sometimes we go to the homes of friends who have older children with smartphones, and these kids have been playing on them in front of our eldest daughter, or wanted to take photos and put filters on them for fun. Even though it's all been age-appropriate, we feel it's important to teach our daughter that if smartphones are not for children, then she can't play on someone else's smartphone either.

This can be tough when we're spending time with friends, and it hasn't always worked out, but we've learnt from our errors and agreed as a parenting couple to speak up much earlier to prevent the kind of situation we don't feel comfortable with. This has meant that at the beginning of a playdate or day out with another family whose children carry smartphones, we speak to the parents in advance and say something like, 'We'd prefer for our daughter not to watch or play on a smartphone. We know your child has one, but if we could keep it out of reach for a couple of hours it would really help us.' On occasion we've also spoken to the child and said something like, 'Our daughter can't play on a smartphone or watch you play on yours. It's OK if that's what you want to do, but we'd be really grateful if you don't do it in front of her.'

Perhaps we're very lucky or have excellent, thoughtful friends, but we've never received pushback from this, and once we've had the conversation the first time, we've never had to repeat it because our friends and their children have always remembered our preference. On one occasion, a child's friend said, 'Wait, I'm not going to have my phone as she's not allowed it yet,' and on another, when we told a child that our daughter couldn't look at Snapchat, she replied, 'If she can't see it, I won't look at it either.'

If as an adult you worry that these conversations are cringey or awkward, please find the courage to have them and let those worries melt away. Children, and their parents who are your good friends, are caring and thoughtful. They'll want to make things safe for you and your child, because at the end of the day it's sharing your company that matters.

I'm not saying it's always going to be this easy, but it can be. You just need to be clear about the expectations you want to set and communicate them clearly to your children in a way that's thoughtful, clear and consistent. This is the baseline, but understanding your child and their existing screen usage, temperament and behaviours will help you implement the delay in a way that works for them. We'll come on to this in Step 2 of the Family Phone Pledge Plan.

Step 2

Understanding your child

Now that you've got a better understanding of your phone habits, how they can impact your child and what they choose to do in the future when they have a smartphone, it's time to look at who your children are. There are no one-size-fits-all approaches, because all children are unique. What works for some children might not work for yours, so it's worth taking the time to understand how your child relates to digital technologies, the effects screen time have on them, and how their temperament, likes, dislikes and unique interests can influence the relationship they develop with the digital world. My hope is that at the end of this section you'll be better informed about who your child is, and possess more tools and greater motivation to begin open and honest conversations about the positive and negative elements of the digital world and smartphone ownership.

Smartphone health check for children

When it comes to your children, although many won't yet have smartphones, they very well might have access to screens of one sort or another. Screens are the gateway to smartphones, and the habits you embed in your homes around screens form the foundation for the expectations, rules and limits you'll most probably set with smartphones. Getting a snapshot of how smartphones are currently being used in your home and the relationships your children are developing with digital media is helpful because it gives you a starting point of where you are now, and might help you reflect on the things you're doing well and any small tweaks that might need to be made.

The below questions are based on the SCREENS-Q questionnaire that looks at screen use and behaviour in children. If your child is old enough (over five), I'd invite you to complete this task with them and for you to subsequently discuss how your scores may be the same or different. Please note the word 'screens' in the questionnaire refers to TVs, tablets, smartphones, computers and any sort of gaming device.

Does your child have screens that live in their bedroom?

- Yes
- No

Does your child own a portable device with access to the internet?

- Yes
- No

Does your child use a screen during meals?

- Yes
- Sometimes (three times a week or less)
- No

Does your child use screens for fun, socialising or entertainment during the week?

- Yes, most nights
- Sometimes (three times a week or less, or on holidays only)
- No

Does your child use screens outside the home when waiting around, such as in a queue?

- Yes
- Sometimes (three times a week or less)
- No

Does your child use screens at bedtime to relax?

- Yes
- Sometimes (three times a week or less, or when in a new environment such as a hotel)?
- No

When your child uses a screen, is it mostly:

A. With adult interaction or an adult actively supervising?
B. With someone around but not always hearing or seeing what they are doing?
C. Independently or alone in another room?

When you join your child in digital interactions, such as watching a film together, do you mostly:

A. Always interact, ask questions and talk about it during and/ or after?
B. Sometimes chat but only related to the content of the film/ game/activity, not for teaching purposes?
C. I never join my child in their digital interaction.

After going online with your child to watch, play or do something, how often do you discuss what you enjoyed about it?

A. We often discuss what we both liked about it.
B. We sometimes discuss it, but sometimes we move on to the next thing.
C. Never. I don't go online with my child.

Scoring: 2 points for yes, 1 point for sometimes, 0 points for no; 0 points for A, 1 point for B, 2 points for C.

The higher the score, the more screen time your child is having in a way that might not be keeping them safe or might be distracting them from real-world experiences. This score does not mean that screen time is necessarily impacting on your child's life, but the score might be a useful point of reference if you choose to make changes to how your child uses screens. A change in the score might help you reflect on how your child is engaging in online and offline interactions.

Phone flags: when to worry

When you think about screens in your home, you might start to wonder how much screen use is too much? There are no age-specific screen-time guidelines backed by science, and no guidelines at all when it comes to children using smartphones.[1] But our children communicate with us all the time. Their behaviour alerts us when things are not OK, and they give us clues when screen time is going well and when they need our help to stop it. When you understand some of the behavioural clues your child is sending out to you, you can take appropriate action. I have summarised the most common signs overleaf as a brief guide to help you. Your child might show some signs in one zone and a few in another. As a precaution, it helps to work on the zone that is 'hotter', so you can shrink the problem before it becomes too engrained and pervasive.

The Family Phone Plan

	Red zone	Yellow zone	Green zone
Signs	Screens are your child's main activity. School grades dip/your child refuses to attend school. Playing with friends only happens online. Limited outdoor exercise or movement. Poor sleep (takes longer to fall asleep and sleeps less overall). When screens are off, emotional outbursts become physical and explosive.	Your child spends more time on screens than most of their friends. It's always a battle when screen time is over. Tearfulness, irritability and tantrums happen shortly after screen time (like they are decompressing or releasing stress). Screens are used as a bribe to get your child to do things as a family or with friends in the real world. You think the balance has shifted, with more online interaction than offline.	Screens are used for educational purposes or entertainment under close supervision. Your child reluctantly ends screen time but it isn't a battle. They can follow limits. Your child chooses to spend time with friends or play over screens. You feel like there's a good balance between online and offline interaction.

What to do	See this as a cry for help. Overusing screens can be a symptom of poor mental health. Engage with your child and share the concerns you have for their well-being. Get curious about what's going on in the real world that screens are distracting from (e.g. bullying/academic difficulties/low self-esteem/ anxiety/peer troubles). Re-establish clear boundaries and expectations with screens. You may need to limit them completely for a while so you can support your child. Consider whether your child may have low mood, depression or suicidal thoughts. Don't panic! Find courage to talk about these topics with them. Naming it will not make it worse, it will give your child permission to speak because they now know you can cope with this information. Seek professional help to support you. (There's no shame in this. You haven't failed your child. You are a good parent whose child is struggling and you can work through this.)	Review your screen-time limits, rules and expectations. Ensure anything you tweak for your child you are doing for your own screens too. Talk to your child about your concerns (e.g. around their mood and/or interaction). Have an open dialogue about what your child does online. Is the content over-stimulating/ stressful/upsetting? Focus on doing more activities as a family in and out of your home without screens.	Set clear expectations, rules and limits around screen time as a whole family. Model good screen use. Keep close supervision of your child when they go on screens. Continue to connect and make plans to engage your child in real-world interactions. .

I hope these 'phone flags' feel reassuring and helpful. In my experience as a clinical psychologist, it's very rare to see children in the 'red zone' without other things happening for them in the real world. Fluctuating between the 'yellow' and 'green' zones is quite common; it's worth checking that you haven't become too lax on the boundaries (during holidays, for example). If you feel you have, then get back on track. Remember that this is just a guide, not a diagnostic tool, and some of your child's behaviour will be influenced by their temperament too.

Understanding your child

The smartphone health check and 'When to worry' table are tools that will help give you a snapshot of where your child is with screens and other digital devices right now. But the key to making the smartphone conversation meaningful to you and your child is to tailor it to their personality. Temperament is an important feature of social and emotional health. The word 'temperament' refers to the way we approach and react to the world, our own personal style that's a part of us from birth. There are three general types of temperaments: easy-going, slow to warm (cautious) and highly active. Easy-going children tend to adjust easily to new situations and environments. Slow-to-warm children are generally observant and calm, and they might need extra time to adjust to new situations. Children with highly active temperaments are often more physical and emotionally feisty, and they approach life with zest.

Knowing your child's temperament is important because it gives you a better understanding of their individual differences. By understanding their temperament, you can learn how to help your child better and it can stop you from blaming yourself for reactions that are normal for your child. Psychologists often think about 'goodness of fit' in relation to a child's temperament and their parents' caregiving style. For example, when a parent who is low on activity and enjoys more quiet and sedentary activities such as reading or crafting has a child who's always on the move and needs a lot of physical and environmental stimulation, it can lead to conflict in the parent–child relationship. Understanding that your child isn't to blame for the levels of activity they need, that it doesn't make you a bad parent if your needs are lower and that finding a compromise is necessary to build your relationship, can create positive change in the parent–child dyad.

Here I am going to focus on 'goodness of fit' between your child's temperament and smartphone technology. How will your child engage with a smartphone and how will they cope with the constant influx of messages? I hope reflecting on this may help you consider how your child might respond to owning a smartphone and allow you to plan how best to support them. There are nine common traits that can help describe a child's temperament and I have summarised these in the table below.[2] Take a few minutes to think about who your child is. Perhaps place a dot of colour or a shape for the typical behaviour that reflects them best in each trait.

Trait	Typical behaviour	The smartphone fit
Activity level: refers to physical gross and fine motor activity (e.g. doing sports or creating art)	**High:** always on the move. Has difficulty sitting still.	May be more likely to get bored of the screens and seek out movement.
	Low: prefers less noise and movement. Seeks out sedentary, quiet activities.	May get swept away for hours easily on a screen.

(Continued overleaf)

Distractibility level: getting easily pulled away from what you are doing by other things around you	**High:** difficulty concentrating. More easily distracted by sounds or sights during activities.	May be more likely to get engrossed in the dynamic and ever-changing content of social media.
	Low: has a high level of concentration, pays attention when engaged in an activity, not easily distracted by sounds or sights.	When engrossed online, might struggle to stop and do something in the real world. May need support to transition from screens into real-life activities.
Intensity: refers to emotional reactivity for positive and negative emotions	**High:** shows intense reactions, both positive and negative.	May be susceptible to seeking out online feedback (e.g. want the likes and the followers). More likely to have explosive behavioural outbursts when boundaries are enforced.
	Low: has muted emotional reactions.	May be less likely to show distress when seeing something upsetting online. Least likely to seek help when something goes wrong.
Regularity: relates to the predictability of biological functions	**High:** predictable appetite and sleep patterns. Thrives on a routine.	May respond well to boundaries and limits that are adhered to consistently. Will form habits quickly (good or bad).
	Low: has unpredictable and irregular appetite and sleep patterns, likewise with bowel movements.	May struggle when boundaries and limits are put in and find it hard to follow through. Habits are harder to form.

Sensitivity: feeling things more strongly, like emotions, sounds, or other people's moods	**High:** sensitive to physical stimuli such as sounds, tastes, touch and temperature. For example, struggles to sleep in a new bed (e.g. on holiday).	May get overstimulated by social media and the constant influx of messages on apps. More vulnerable to feeling anxious and having poor sleep.
	Low: not sensitive to physical stimuli. Can easily fall asleep anywhere and enjoys exploring new things (e.g. new foods are interesting rather than scary).	May thrive on stimulation and seek out more entertaining or exciting content. At risk of finding harmful, age-inappropriate content due to their huge curiosity.
Approachability: a person's initial response to new places, situations or things	**High:** keen to approach new situations or people.	More likely to explore social networking and view content that stimulates them.
	Low: slow to warm and hesitant when faced with new situations, people or things.	More likely to go online for social interaction as it takes away the awkward and sensory aspects of face-to-face interaction.
Adaptability: how easily one adjusts to changes and transitions	**High:** transitions easily from activities and situations.	Likely to be highly independent and resistant to control. May find following limits with screens and smartphones difficult unless they have a say in it.
	Low: needs time to transition to new activities or situations.	Will engage best when given the time to understand rules and expectations. Having a plan in place may be helpful.

(Continued overleaf)

Persistence: the extent to which you can keep going with something, even when it's hard or takes time	**High:** continues with a task in the face of obstacles and doesn't get easily frustrated.	May be more likely to bypass the rules and go behind your back if the rules are too strict or punitive.
	Low: moves on to a new task when faced with obstacles. Gets frustrated easily.	May get anxious, irritated and frustrated with messages and comments. More likely to struggle getting off a screen and have emotional outbursts.
Mood: how feelings such as happiness, sadness, calm or anger stick around and are expressed outwardly	**High:** reacts to the world in a positive way and is generally cheerful.	May reap more benefits of going online and socialising with friends and family when done well.
	Low: observant and more serious. Tends to be thoughtful about new situations.	May be vulnerable to the social element of smartphones, and prefer it to socialising face to face.

Look at the spread of dots or shapes you have annotated as a good fit for your child and notice the picture it paints of them in the online world with a smartphone. How does it offer you ideas of where you need to place greater focus, such as building real-world friendships or concentrating on social skills to protect them when they get online?

It's impossible to neatly fit a child into any box, but understanding your child's temperament is something you do know, although you might never have thought about it in quite this way. Temperament changes as children grow, develop and acquire social skills, but overall there are some aspects that remain stable throughout our lifetime.

For those children who tend to be easy or flexible, it might help to know that they are less likely to demand attention and make their needs or distress known. It's therefore important to encourage them to seek help and communicate their feelings. Building a relationship with you that feels secure and trusting is essential to keeping them safe online.

For highly active and feisty children, it can help to know that the intense emotions and reactions they have when screen time ends are not a reflection of being 'naughty' or 'bad', but simply an aspect of their temperament. These children do best when they're given control, and they need a lot of physical activity and movement to balance the time spent engaging on a screen. They respond best to calm interventions that don't threaten or punish them, so that their emotional reactivity is dampened rather than provoked to escalate.

Children who are slow to warm and cautious may benefit from predictable routines and tight boundaries with screens and smartphones. Some research has found that children with cautious temperaments are most likely to struggle with smartphone use; they tend to engage with smartphones more than most, can find it difficult to regulate their emotions after using them and persist in using them despite experiencing negative physical, psychological and social consequences.[3]

Understanding your child's temperament is important to help you consider the individual skills you'll need to adopt in your approach when delaying smartphones, answering their questions and engaging their willingness to follow the boundaries and limits that you set.

As your child grows up and moves towards the teen years, you'll again have to explore 'who' your child is becoming, looking at them through a different lens. This means becoming curious about what life is like in their teen world while withholding your adult judgements and assumptions, listening to their experiences with openness and a willingness to learn, and validating that what they are feeling and how they are reacting to experiences, which are often firsts, is real and understandable. You must keep an open dialogue about your children's digital lives and take interest in what they do online, what their friends are up to and the language they use to communicate with their peers in the real world.

Understanding your child isn't just fundamental to building a connected and trusting relationship with them. It's also about becoming aware of the areas you may need to focus on, how best to communicate your family's rules and limits, and how to support them during this period of waiting for a smartphone. This is what we'll explore next.

Step 3
Open and honest dialogue

Children naturally compare themselves with others, and when they see everyone else in their age bracket with a smartphone, it can create a strong desire for them to get one too. This group mindset is a normal part of childhood. To want to have the same things as others so as not to stand out as different is a natural human tendency that's important in childhood development; children learn to navigate social situations by observing and aligning themselves with their peers, understanding subconsciously that being part of a group offers safety, support and belonging. The desire to be accepted by their peers can influence children's behaviour and decision-making and it enables them to develop a sense of self and identity.[1] It appears no different to children wanting the same trendy drinking cup or the latest trainers that all their friends have. But smartphones are a little different, because children rightfully worry that being excluded from online conversations with their friends will mean that they'll miss out, and can leave them feeling rejected and isolated too.

Peer norm influence is a theory that states: 'When a certain behaviour becomes the norm within a peer group, it will exert pressure to conform to this norm.'[2] We know that over recent years smartphone ownership has become the norm for teens, one that becomes almost universal around eleven years of age, coinciding with the transition to secondary school. It makes sense, therefore, that when children get closer to that age, they'll push for a smartphone so that they align with their peers, maintain friendships and have a sense of belonging. This is why delaying smartphones is no small feat, because it takes courage as parents to say 'not yet' and go against the norm. But this is where Step 4 of the Family Phone Plan comes in. If you and all your children's friends' parents sign the pledge on page 154 and make a committed promise to delay smartphones, your child will not be missing out on conforming to the norm, since you might revolutionise what the norm with smartphones in teenage years is.

So rather than being a rite of passage into secondary school as it is now, perhaps the norm becomes 'not yet', or 'after you turn thirteen'. Perhaps the norm becomes a little more sensible and developmentally appropriate, where we're consciously aware that smartphones are a privilege, and there's no automatic right to own one. If we all commit to doing this, it might well be the greatest decision of our parenting generation.

I know that saying 'not yet' to phones sounds simple, but the reality of doing it is harder. In this third step of the Family Phone Plan, I'll give you the tools to develop your own road map to delaying the introduction of smartphones in your home, offer scripts and tools to help you clearly lay out the expectation of delaying phones, and show you how to open up a dialogue with your children in a way that will foster connection. Finding the words with which to explain to your child why you're delaying smartphones and answer their questions can be hard, so I'm offering you scripts to guide you. These are not to be learnt by heart. They're simply ideas and thought-starters so you can find your own words to have these conversations with your child in a way that suits their temperament and unique personality.

It's also important to make sure the conversation you have with your child about smartphones is age-appropriate. The best way to say 'not yet' is going to sound different if your child is five years old as opposed to ten. It's worth understanding the developmental stage your children are in and accommodating to it so your conversations are as effective as they can be.

Toddlers and preschoolers (two to five years)

When children younger than two see you with a smartphone they won't understand what it is or possess the language to ask for it. Around the age of two or so you might start to see your child reaching out for your phone and asking to play with it, look at your wallpaper photo or begin to ask to 'watch it'. While preschool children tend to have expanding vocabularies, they still need explanations to be as simple as possible as their brain hasn't developed the ability to understand abstract concepts such as the value of money or the duration of time. That's why you'll often notice children around this age ask repeatedly 'when' something is going to happen or ask you 'Is it Friday yet?' when they know they're due to have a playdate with their preferred friend on that day.

This is a great period of time to be a positive role model and set a strong example by ensuring you follow tight rules around smartphones, especially when you're with your child. You might like to put your phone in a different room and away from your person when you play with your child, for example, or ensure that if it beeps or buzzes you don't allow it to interfere in any interactions between you and your child. See your child as a first priority and your smartphone as the last.

Whenever you need to say something, use simple language and stay honest: 'Smartphones are not toys; when you're older, you'll be allowed to use one.'

Primary school children (six to ten years)

Children's vocabularies during this age span are expanding rapidly. With some prompting and support they can show critical-thinking skills, and they're in a vitally important stage for social skills and friendship development. It's during these years that you're most likely to get asked lots of questions about smartphones, things like 'When will I get a smartphone?' and 'How come you're allowed to have one but I'm not?' It's a good time to be clear about the things you want to teach your child about smartphones, to keep role-modelling the behaviours you want them to learn and to set expectations with calm confidence, clarity and warmth. Most children this age don't have smartphones yet, but they will have an innate curiosity about the world, so when they ask about them provides a golden opportunity to lay the foundations of the family phone plan you want to set in place.

As early as feels appropriate, let your child know that you'll be delaying smartphones until they're thirteen years old. I suggest the first few times you let this drop in as a breezy comment. Something like, 'You won't get a smartphone until you are thirteen, but you won't need one before then anyway.' And if they ask you the question explicitly, keep it clear and simple: 'Smartphones weren't created for children. They need you to be at least thirteen to have the skills and maturity to use them responsibly and safely.'

This is a great age to get your children involved in the Family Phone Pledge (which we'll go into next). Listen to their views, opinions and ideas, especially about the things they want you to do less of with your smartphone. Make sure they feel a part of co-creating family phone rules in your home, rather than feel like they're having this 'done' to them.

If you feel a phone is needed for your child during the primary school years so that they're contactable and able to contact you, perhaps consider a mobile phone without 'smart' capabilities so they can stay connected via phone call or message but not have unfettered access to the internet.

Tweens (eleven to thirteen years)

At this age children have become acutely aware of smartphones. Many children will now have them as they head to secondary school, and their questions will get more specific and complex. It's important not to dismiss your children's questions, even if they feel incessant. See them simply as a cry for understanding. Your child will need you to see that feeling left out is hard, so having you take the time to talk, empathise and support them through these years is important. This is the hardest period of 'waiting' for your child, and for you too.

Make sure you clearly share your reasons for delaying smartphones, and do so with softness, not harshness or frustration: 'Smartphones can distract you from your schoolwork and the internet has lots of risks that might make you feel overwhelmed. We want you to focus on building good digital skills and healthy habits first. One day you will get a smartphone but not yet.'

Empathise with their situation and normalise this experience: 'I know it's hard to wait, and lots of your friends are waiting too. My job as your parent is to keep you safe, and I want to hear what waiting is like for you. Let's keep talking.'

Teens (fourteen to sixteen years)

This is most likely the age when your child will get a smartphone, and they'll be following your family's phone rules and boundaries. Your job now is to consolidate the relationship you've built with your child, listening to their views and experiences so you can negotiate the rule and continue to be the 'go-to' person with whom they feel they can share their thoughts, feelings and experiences. It's about remaining the adult who will protect and support them, being a helpful sounding board and guide when they need help, rather than someone who lectures, punishes, shames or rejects.

When talking about smartphones, acknowledge their feelings and offer praise and encouragement for what they do well: 'You've been waiting a long time for a smartphone and we are really proud of the things you've been learning. Thank you for always coming to us to share the apps you are using. We love learning with you about new things like this.'

State your position when necessary: 'We need you to show us that you can follow the Family Phone Pledge rules around phones and digital screens. At the moment, we're still having too many arguments during the week about how much time you spend online, and that's just with your mobile phone and your laptop.'

Be sure also to shower your children with empathy. Although they're now older, that doesn't mean that learning to live with a smartphone and following the boundaries you've maintained all this time isn't difficult: 'We need to feel that you're ready to carry such an expensive, luxury item in your pocket and know how to use it well. It's normal that you find this hard. Let's keep working on things together . . . we'll get there.'

We have a responsibility as parents and loving adults to practise what we preach. Our children will be influenced to live with smartphones through what we do with them more than what we tell them to do. Make sure you follow the pledge rules so that what you're doing is not just delaying smartphone ownership, but teaching lifelong balance.

The best way to say 'not yet' to smartphones

Toddlers and preschoolers (two to five years)

For you. Be a positive role model and set a strong example by ensuring you follow well-defined rules around smartphones, especially when your child is with you. This might involve putting it in a different room and away from your person when you're engaging in play, or ensuring that if it beeps or buzzes you don't allow it to interfere in the interactions you have with your child. See your child as the first priority and your smartphone as the last.

When you need to say something. Use simple language and stay honest: 'Smartphones are not toys. When you're older you'll be allowed to use one.'

Primary school children (six to ten years)

Set clear expectations. Tell them early on that you'll be delaying smartphones until they're thirteen years old or more: 'Smartphones were not created for children. They need you to be at least thirteen to have the skills and maturity to use them responsibly and safely.'

Sign the Family Phone Pledge. Get them involved in the pledge, listening to their views, opinions and ideas, especially about the things they want you to do less of with your smartphone. Make sure they feel a part of this rather than that it's something that's being 'done' to them.

Offer an alternative if needed. You might like to consider giving them a mobile phone without the 'smart' capabilities of the internet so they can make and receive calls and messages. Think about this option if you feel your child needs to have a means to be contactable or to contact you.

Tweens (eleven to thirteen years)

Share your why. 'Smartphones can distract you from your schoolwork and the internet has lots of risks that might make you feel overwhelmed. We want you to focus on building good digital skills and healthy habits first.'

Empathise with their situation and normalise this experience. 'I know it's hard to wait, and lots of your friends are waiting too. My job as your parent is to keep you safe. Let's keep talking.'

Teens (fourteen to sixteen years)

Acknowledge their feelings. 'You've been waiting a long time for a smartphone and we're really proud of the things you've been learning.'

State your position. 'We need you to show us that you can follow the pledge rules around phones and digital screens. At the moment, we're still having too many arguments during the week, and that's just with your mobile phone and your laptop.'

Empathise. 'I know it feels like you've been waiting forever, but we need to feel confident that you're ready to carry such an expensive, luxury item in your pocket and know

> how to use it well. Let's keep working on things together . . .
> we'll get there, I promise.'

How to answer your child's questions

In response to your explanation, your child will most likely have lots of questions. It's both a privilege and a responsibility to answer them. When a question puts you in one of those 'uh oh' moments, I want you to know: this is great! You might not know how to answer your child's questions, but the fact they've come to you says a huge amount about your relationship. They trust you, and you're absolutely the best person to answer their question, even if you don't feel it right now. So, have faith in yourself and remember, when a child asks you a question, they've just sent you the gift that says, 'I trust you.'

The most powerful thing you can do is listen to your child, so take some time to process the question, even if it means sitting in an awkward silence for a few seconds. If you find yourself reacting internally – heart beating faster, adrenaline pumping, feeling anxious, mind racing – know that that is just a natural response. Do what you need to do to ground yourself for a moment: take some time for a few deep breaths, step out of the room and say, 'This is important, I want to talk to you. I just need a moment,' drink some water and return to the conversation. Learn to tolerate this discomfort so you can gather your thoughts and take a breath.

Children tend to have formulated an answer in their minds before they ask you something, and when it comes to smartphones it's usually that you're going to tell them that they're never going to get one. This might be correct – for now – but if you reply right away, you might say something you're going to regret. You might want to say 'no' immediately, or tell them 'never', and this might feel like the truth at this particular time, but if you shut down the conversation like this, you'll put yourself in a battle of power with your child. You can stay in charge while showing your child that you're willing to listen to their wants and wishes, and this might help your child not go behind your back looking at things on others' smartphones without telling you. So instead, get curious, ask questions to understand them better, and if you don't know what to tell them, say so. Show your child you're willing to listen, even if you choose to respond with, 'No, not yet.'

During the conversation, allow your child to use whatever words come up without correcting them and try to use their language too. It doesn't really matter how it all sounds right now, it's more important to 'get it out' and give your child permission not to think too hard about the delivery. Sometimes children will preface this sort of conversation with something like, 'Please don't get angry with me . . .' and that's your sign to regulate yourself and try to send a message to your child that says, 'You can tell me anything. Nothing will scare me. I am here.' Make sure you open the door to communication in these moments because it's when you know more about your child's experiences, thoughts and feelings that you can protect them best. You don't have to have all the answers on the spot. If there are things outside of your comfort zone, give them assurance that you'll find the help they need.

Why can't I have a phone until I'm at least thirteen?

Even if you set out your vision of what's going to happen, it's probable that your child will come up with questions such as 'Why can't I have a phone before I'm at least thirteen?' or 'How come Susie has a smartphone if they're not for children?' I won't lie, these are tough ones to answer, but you can reply in ways that aren't combative. Try instead to be compassionate and thoughtful while confidently saying, 'Not yet.'

Doing this comes with the implication that you've got clear boundaries and limits about the idea of delaying smartphones, and that you're not just doing it because 'someone' (including me) has told you it's a good idea. Once you feel deep within that delaying smartphones is the right choice for your child's safety within the context of your family dynamics, the limit feels easier to action. It's all the easier if you already have other similar boundaries in place. One rule in our house is that our children are in bed by 8 p.m., so by that time we ensure they're in pyjamas, their teeth are brushed and they're tucked up in bed so the lights can go off. We also have a rule not to give our children pop or sugary drinks, so our limit is not to buy any in our weekly food shop so that we never have any on offer.

When you can sit comfortably within your parenting authority to make these sorts of rules, you can answer your child's plea of 'Why can't I have a phone before I am thirteen?' with a lot less emotion and a lot more care. This will involve:

- **Giving your child eye contact when they ask you this question.** Stop what you're doing and pay attention – you must value this conversation if you're going to give your child the message that it matters.

- **Expressing your limit when you reply.** You *must* believe in your boundary to do this with calm confidence.

So rather than taking an authoritarian stance, which might sound like, 'Ugh, how many times have you asked me this question? You won't be getting a smartphone until you're at least thirteen and that's final, OK?' or tentatively adopting a wobbly, permissive stance that shows you're shaky about your limit, which may sound like, 'Because I said so, OK? Please don't keep asking me for a phone. You know I hate upsetting you. I *am* sorry . . . I just don't think it's right,' come through with a confident, authoritative stance.

This should sound more like: 'You're thinking about smartphones again, huh? I get it. It's really hard to have to wait until you're thirteen. But you know, smartphones are not for children. They're a big responsibility and they give you access to lots of apps and sites that are unsafe for children your age. I can't let you have a phone before you're at least thirteen because it's my job as a parent to keep you safe. Having a smartphone would put you at risk, and that's not worth doing right now. It's OK if you don't like this decision, and you're allowed to be angry with me, but you know my answer is "not yet".'

Focus on emotional regulation

This is for you as much as your child. You must learn to exhale slowly, have a cold glass of water to hand, or even shake it off if you need to so that you can respond with calm confidence and sturdy leadership when your child kicks off at your answer. Show your child that their emotions are not scary to you, that you can tolerate their distress. If what you see is a big explosion of anger and tears, hold back from speaking about it. The most powerful thing you can do is bring calm to your child's storm. Wait. It. Out.

This doesn't mean you ignore your child or show up in a Zen state; it means you let them release their emotions – which will help to regulate them – and delineate a boundary if need be. This might sound like, 'I get why you are angry/frustrated/upset about this. You're allowed to feel this way. I can't hear what you want to say to me when you're like this so let's take a break. When you're ready, I've got a big hug waiting for you.'

It's important to show your child that their feelings matter to you, that you're not afraid of them and that you want to keep talking about it. And it's OK to set a limit around their behaviour if what your child does is use hurtful words or gets physical. Your child's reaction is their emotional response to the limit you set; it doesn't mean you've got it wrong or that you're harming them. Some children will have much bigger emotional responses to this than others – it's to do with their temperament and the strength of their desire to have a smartphone. Allow your child to have their feelings, and remain confident in your decision.

Hold the limit

Wait it out and delay giving your child a smartphone until their brains and hearts are sufficiently developed to cope with the deluge of information these devices can access, and until they possess the impulse control and critical-thinking skills to stay safe when they're bombarded with inappropriate content. Your child might not like it, or agree, but it's not your job to give them lots of information to justify your decision or try to convince them that you're right. It's your job to do what you feel is needed to keep them safe. It's OK to say you'll wait until they're at least thirteen, and then, when the time comes, choose to delay this a bit longer if you don't think your child is ready or if there isn't a good reason to get them a smartphone yet. And if for any reason you bring this forward, pay attention to what has led you to make this choice. Who has influenced you in this? Are *you* making the decision of centring your child's needs, or is someone or something else? Have you considered whether any of the alternatives are viable, safer options?

There are lots of reasons why you might find saying 'not yet' difficult. Perhaps you and your partner have different views, and getting aligned in your parenting is hard, or maybe you've got a strong desire to be liked by your children, and coping with their disappointment feels unbearable. It's also possible that you were parented in a strict way and you now want to change the narrative by showing you're able to hear their opinions and stay on their side.

It helps, I find, to know that firm boundaries and limits are part of loving discipline. Boundaries don't have to be controlling, threatening, shaming, or come with punishments and threats. They can come with empathy, understanding and a deep knowledge that protecting your child is your job, even when it's hard to do. When you delay smartphones, you're firmly on your child's side. It might not feel like that to your child, because conforming with their peer group is deeply important to them, but as they get older, perhaps when they get a smartphone, perhaps when they become parents themselves, they'll understand that what you did was with their best interests at heart. In the same way that children battle for freedoms that they're not ready to have yet – whether it's going on a sleepover, visiting the cinema unsupervised with friends or attending that 'cool' house party everyone else is allowed to go to – if you deem it isn't right for your child, dig deep and find the courage to say 'no'.

In case you need it, here are some empathic lines you could say to your child when they feel anger, upset, disappointment or frustration about the fact that getting a smartphone feels light years away from being a reality. You could say:

- 'I understand that you really want a smartphone. I'm sorry waiting is so hard.'
- 'It sounds like you're feeling left out because you don't have a smartphone yet. Tell me what you are missing out on, I want to understand.'
- 'I can see that you're upset/angry about this decision, and it's OK to feel that way.'
- 'I know it's tough when you have to wait for something you really want. It feels like the day will never come, but I promise, it will. Just not yet.'
- 'It's OK to feel frustrated. Waiting is a really hard thing to do. Do you want to talk about what we can do while you wait?'
- 'I'm sorry that this decision is making you feel upset. Being a parent is really hard because I often have to make decisions that you don't like, and I don't like upsetting you. But my job is to protect you, and I'd rather you were upset

with me right now than upset, shaken or worried about
something that you saw on a smartphone.'

- 'I know you think it's unfair. There are so many things that
you cannot do yet. I remember feeling like you do when I
was your age too. Trust me, you'll get a smartphone one day,
and I'll be there to support you when you do.'

The art of waiting

Delaying smartphones is forcing children to learn patience and
delayed gratification – two life skills that smartphones are really
good at stealing away from them. We have to be realistic that doing
this is never going to be easy. Delaying smartphones doesn't mean
that your child will stop having meltdowns, that there will be fewer
emotional outbursts and less conflict or irritation in your home
because smartphones are not around. Children are still developing
their emotional and social skills, which are nowhere near maturity
(that won't happen until their mid-twenties), and they have very
poor impulse control because their brains aren't yet able to buffer
impulsivity very well. To me, these are all reasons that support
delaying smartphones, but you can do more than just say 'not yet'.
What follows are some strategies that can help you support your
child in learning how to wait.

Encourage and support your child's interests

This isn't about overscheduling extracurricular activities, but
more about finding opportunities for your child to engage in

interests and develop skills in areas that they feel passionate about. Perhaps it's a team activity like hockey, football, cricket, choir, drama or scouts. Maybe it's an independent activity like tennis, karate, swimming, art, cooking or playing an instrument. From eight years onwards, giving children opportunities to build identities outside of school and the network of peers that they've met there is a really positive thing to do. When children mix with peers from other schools, socio-economic backgrounds and communities, all with a common interest or goal, it builds their identity, offering them an outlet for self-expression, creativity and exploration that can develop their confidence and self-esteem. It's good for them to have a space away from the peer group they see every day, a different group of people to get to know and connect with. This gives them a sense of belonging to a group of children who share the same passion. It's social networking in real life.

Protect time for fun and play

Are you a parent who finds play hard? You're not alone and it's not totally your fault. Once our brains mature and we spend less of our days doing playful, enjoyable things, our creative juices can dry up. Adulting is sometimes no fun at all. But when it comes to parenting, we must protect pockets of time to play with our children, to find our silly side and join them in their world. So this is your cue to put your phone down, switch off your laptop and plan some fun times with your children.

Maybe you can create a regular 'games night' every Friday, or plan different Sunday challenges with a leaderboard (this can be very alluring for those who love a competition). There are tons of great games that don't need a smartphone. Some family favourites of ours include UNO, Poo Bingo, Yahtzee, Bananagrams, Ticket to Ride, and our all-time favourite, Carcassonne (once you get into this game, you'll have to place a limit on how many rounds you play or you'll be up all night . . . you've been warned!). Play builds connection and also helps to develop important skills such as emotional regulation, impulse control and problem-solving. Importantly, playing games is a form of bonding, and these moments are like small deposits in your child's love bank. If you want your child to feel seen, safe and soothed by you, make sure you make time to play.

Keep talking about smartphones

Your child might not be allowed their own smartphone, but they can learn a lot by watching and understanding what you do. Children are often fascinated by smartphones because they have a special, nearly magical quality. You can break the spell by engaging in conversations about what you do on yours. This might feel odd because it's an unfamiliar thing to do. Most adults engage in the online world in silence, as they do when reading a novel, yet most of what we do doesn't need to feel special, secretive or even private. Take a deep breath, and next time you pull your phone out and your children are around, try to talk about what you do on it. For your child, the experience of hearing you say what you're doing on your phone makes the experience less detached, mysterious and appealing. It's quite dull for them to know you're adding food items to the shopping list or replying to Aunt Bessie's message.

Of course, there are times when doing something on your phone and sharing it will lead to your child saying something like, 'Oh! Can I see?' When a text message appears and your child is around, let them know it's a written message from work, family or friends. If you get sent a photo and it's appropriate to show them, do so, and use it as an opportunity to talk about what is and isn't appropriate to send online. The experiences you have on your phone can become learning opportunities about the digital world. You obviously don't have to do this for every message you receive or everything you do online, but if you try to regularly do it, you'll be filling your child with knowledge while they learn patience.

Offer digital experiences where possible

We can't completely protect our children from the digital world, and in any case it's a world they'll need to learn to inhabit and develop the appropriate skills for as they approach adulthood. Try to find ways to alleviate some of the downsides of not having a smartphone when your children's friends get one. This might be allowing them to video-call friends via a tablet under your supervision, using an 'un-smart' phone for calls and texts when they're away from home and at certain agreed hours in your home, or letting them enjoy gaming online with their friends on closed digital platforms where you can have an oversight of what they play, who with and for how long. None of these things are the same as owning a smartphone, but when you offer your child safe ways to connect with friends online, you give them the opportunity to build skills and lessen the social anxiety that can develop when children feel socially isolated from their peers.

Find your circle

This one is for you, the parent, but it will also support your child. Find a parenting circle in which others are delaying phones too, often your closest friends and the parents around your child. A few years ago, it might have seemed like you would be alone in this venture, but now lots of parents have started to wake up to the potential risks of smartphones for children, and the momentum is growing. Some parents may have already given older children a smartphone and fear being rejected by those who are strongly in favour of delaying them. Try to be an inclusive and compassionate parent who's open to anyone who wants to consider this idea with you.

We are the first generation of parents having to navigate the choppy seas of the internet with very few safety floats to support us. We're all going to make mistakes along the way, and that's OK. It doesn't make us 'bad parents', it makes us humans trying to do our best and learn as we go. If we can all lean in and try to cultivate relationships with each other that are based on curiosity, understanding and respect, then perhaps we can model to our children what the power of real-life connection can really do and possibly change the course of young lives. We'll revisit the importance of finding a community around the issue of smartphones in Step 5, Involving others.

Step 4

Join the Family Phone Pledge

Being a parent is often hard and can feel especially challenging when you're pushing against smartphone culture. I created the Family Phone Pledge to help you feel empowered in your decision and model to your children the fact that you're not just the gatekeeper of their well-being, you're also safeguarding real-world experiences for the whole family.

Now it's time to take all you've learnt and thought about so far and write your own Family Phone Pledge. In this chapter I'll guide you through the process and show you how to engage your family – after all, your best chance of embedding the Family Phone Pledge successfully is if everyone feels heard and involved. Remember, the pledge isn't just for a week or a month or a few years. It's hopefully going to ground and support you up until your child is old enough to get a smartphone, and when they do, it might help you to consolidate some of the good habits you've been building in your home.

Negotiating the Family Phone Pledge

Once you feel confident that you want to write your own Family Phone Pledge, the next step is to invite your child to lay out your expectations. The pledge works best when you all agree the expectations and rules around smartphones in your home and you all agree to sign it as a symbol of your commitment to each other. When children are little – below the age of five – it's OK to include them in the pledge and let them hear the conversation, but their input might be very limited, and that's OK. All they need to know is that you're delaying smartphones until the age of at least thirteen.

Setting the scene

Like all important conversations, take the time to think about when the right time is to have this talk and where will be most comfortable. For example, doing this on an evening after school, jammed between dinner and bathtime, might feel rushed and unsatisfactory. Doing it on a Saturday evening might give you more time, but if your child has big feelings about the pledge, it might escalate and make bedtime difficult or leave them struggling to fall asleep with questions rolling round in their minds.

I'd suggest that a morning when you haven't got many plans is a good time to have this conversation, share the pledge and open up dialogue. You want to pre-empt the possibility that your child will have lots of feelings and give them the space for this to be

OK. And you want to allow your child to have the time to digest the information and ask questions that you may or may not be able to fully answer, but you can begin to.

It's worth knowing that when big topics like this are broached, it often takes more than one conversation, so your first Family Phone Pledge discussion is simply that – the first of many on the topic. Don't worry if you feel like you're flailing around with words or are out of your depth answering your child's questions. You'll have lots of chances to get better at this, and importantly, the pledge is about affirming your decision to delay smartphones until your child is at least thirteen. The more this becomes a confident statement from you, the easier it will be to get curious about your child's questions. Because rather than seeing them as challenges to your authority, you will understand that your child is simply making sense of an adult decision that they have little awareness of (just like they might ask why they cannot drink alcohol or get in front of the wheel of your car).

How to fill out your pledge

This is the Family Phone Pledge template, and I've filled it out with some examples of things you may wish to include. Over the next few pages we'll talk about how you and your family can fill it out together. Please note the pledge refers to children in the plural, so amend the pledge accordingly if it only refers to one child.

The Family Phone Pledge

We are (names of adults and children) _____

_____

Our family values are (examples):

- Kindness and respect
- Responsibility
- Honesty
- Creativity

Family photo/coat of arms/image that represents YOU

When we're home, our smartphones will be safe in the daytime and overnight when not in use (e.g. charging in the kitchen/lounge/utility room).

As adults, we agree to:

- Delay giving our children a smartphone until they're at least thirteen years old.
- Supervise older children who have access to smartphones and make it our responsibility to ensure they're keeping younger siblings safe too.
- Be a safe, trusting adult by:
  - always listening when things go wrong online.
  - showing willingness to understand and learn.
  - never blaming or punishing.
- Stay connected to parents/friends/family who support this pledge and regularly meet together.
- Honour regular family meetings to discuss and review our family phone pledge and make changes as needed.

As older children, when we get a phone we pledge to:

- Protect younger siblings and their friends from accessing smartphones.
- Understand that smartphones are a responsibility, not a right, and showing we can use them safely is important.
- Stay safe online by:
  - only accessing the apps and content agreed with our parents.
  - talking to our parents about what we do online.
  - getting help when we need it.
- Show we are responsible enough to have a phone by:
  - following the house phone rules.
  - keeping our phones safe.
  - only using it in spaces and places we are allowed to.

As a family we pledge to spend time together every week

Agreed family phone-free zones (examples):

- Bedrooms
- Mealtimes
- Family quality time (game night)

Communal areas where phones and screens can be used, without headphones (examples):

- Lounge
- Dining room
- Car

People who are part of this pledge as sources of support and inspiration are (names):

_____

_____

As a family we pledge to value each other more than our phones. When we're with others and reach for our phones, we agree to talk about what we do in the digital world so no one feels ignored or excluded.

- Protect screen-free time.
- Protect screen-free zones.
- Keep learning digital skills together.
- Show curiosity and acceptance about digital interests. We will not mock, tease or dismiss others' interests online in the same way that we don't do this in the real world.
- Have an open password policy as a family (e.g. all use the same password to unlock smartphones).

As parents we pledge to not overreact when you see or find something online that upsets, disturbs or frightens you or someone you know. Our job is to protect you and keep you safe and we take this very seriously.

As children we pledge to talk to you or a safe adult when we see or get sent something that upsets or frightens us or any of our friends. Our job is to sound the alarm to protect ourselves and those we love.

We accept that doing all the above will take time and commitment.

We will make mistakes and can keep working on this together.

We will remind each other of our family pledge in ways that are **kind, respectful** and **positive** to make the presence of smartphones something that brings us joy ☺, rather than something that makes us feel bad ☹.

Signed:

Parents   **Children**

The pledge contains sections that are non-negotiable, such as the age you'll delay your child from smartphone ownership. But there are other areas of the pledge where your child can and should have a voice. These can include:

- our family values
- agreed family phone-free zones
- communal areas where phones and screens can be used
- family activities (online and offline)
- people who are part of the pledge as sources of support and inspiration
- our family agreements

If you want your child to be a willing participant in the pledge, allow them to have a voice in these areas that are creating a family ethos around smartphones. Allow them to tell you (and any older siblings with phones) what is and isn't OK to do with phones in your home. This may be confronting and uncomfortable, but as the only members of the house without a smartphone, it's worth considering that their experience is the best reflection of your smartphone habits – and yes, it's likely you have embedded some bad habits without even realising it!

The initial Family Phone Pledge conversation

Here's an example of what this might sound like:[*]

> We want to talk to you about smartphones and some of the things we've been thinking about lately. When we got our smartphones, nobody taught us to use them, we just learnt as we went along – and we've made plenty of mistakes along the way. Lots of parents like us have started to realise that although smartphones are great and can be really useful, they also steal a lot of our time and get in the way of our relationships. For example, we're so used to checking our phones we sometimes allow them to interrupt the fun we're having with you or the conversations we have with each other. Have you noticed that? Yeah, we're sorry those things happened. We think it's wrong and we want to change these bad habits we have with our smartphones.
>
> A lot of parents started to give smartphones to their children as a way to stay in touch with them or keep them safe. But after doing lots of reading, many parents like us have started to realise that smartphones were never made for children, because they give access to the internet, which has all sorts of things in it, including dangerous content and mean comments from people. That is why we've decided that we'll not be getting you a smartphone until you are at least thirteen, which is the age most apps on the internet say

* Note: I've deliberately kept the specifics of what children might find online via their smartphone vague here. Depending on the age of your child, you may want to be specific about some of things they could encounter on a smartphone – like porn, self-harm and violence, for example. There is more information on how to have these conversations on page 215.

it's OK for children to join, and when we think you might have the maturity and skills to cope a bit better with what happens online.

But even when you get a smartphone, there will be rules you'll have to follow to show us you're responsible enough to use it both inside and outside our home. These rules will also apply to us, and to show you we're committed to keeping you safe and care deeply about our family, we want to sign the Family Phone Pledge.

[Show the pledge to everyone present and look at it together.]

This is who we are as a family, and what we think our values are. These are the foundations of what we think helps our family flow smoothly, the things we appreciate and care about (see family values box). Which do you think are a good fit for us?

Family values

Here's a brief list of family values that you may wish to discuss and think about for your Family Phone Pledge. Pick two or three values that align best with your family. Invite your children to help you choose these; it will help them align more strongly with the pledge and what you all stand for as a family.

Honesty: being open, truthful and acting with integrity

Kindness: showing care and thoughtfulness towards others

Responsibility: taking care of things and taking ownership of our actions

Respect: treating each other with courtesy, consideration and equality

---

Forgiveness: letting go of grudges and understanding that everyone makes mistakes

Patience: managing frustration and listening with compassion

Generosity: giving without expecting anything in return

Working as a team: not hurting each other's property or our own, and working to solve problems and support each other

Family time: making space for quality moments together to build memories and have fun

This is where we pledge to keep our smartphones when we are at home and don't need to use them. Rather than carrying them on our person, we pledge to switch the ring tone on in case we need to be contacted and leave them apart from us. We were thinking _____ might be a good place to leave our phones. What do you think? Do you have any ideas?

These are the pledges *we* make as parents.

[Read them out. Discuss. Allow for questions.]

These are the pledges *you* make when you get a smartphone (or for older siblings, 'now you have a smartphone').

[Read them. Negotiate. Allow for questions and feelings. Take a pause here if you need to and come back to discuss the pledge later, perhaps on another day. It's OK for this process to take time. A well-thought-out and negotiated Family Phone Pledge is more likely to stick than one that's rushed and quickly signed without alignment between all of you.]

The pledge is also about making sure we spend quality family time without our smartphones getting in the way. What kind of things would you like us to do more as a family with and without screens?

[It's OK to include a weekly film night or a family video-game challenge. Engaging in digital worlds with your children is fun and can be a healthy opportunity to teach them that true connection can exist alongside screens, not just inside them.]

Real-world and digital activities – some ideas

A few favourites to start you off with. If you don't use screen-based activities much, or you don't protect family time offline, it can be hard to think of what this might look like. This is just to start you off and is by no means a comprehensive list! Your ideas are likely to be better than mine, but give this a try:

Real-world activities

- Games night (Carcassonne, UNO, Bananagrams, Ticket to Ride)
- Home baking (cupcakes, banana bread)
- Having a 'home spa' (nails, facials, feet pampering)
- Creative making together (building a Lego *Star Wars* set, making bracelets, origami)
- Nature walks
- Cycling, skating, doing a sport together (running, tennis, swimming)
- Completing puzzles (crosswords or word searches)

Screen-based activities

- Family film night. Commonsensemedia.org curates film reviews that might be a useful guide to assess appropriateness better than 'age restrictions', which are not based on content.
- Watch a weekly series or show together.
- Play videos games. *Wii Sports, Super Mario Kart* and *The Legend of Zelda* are our favourites. You can go to askaboutgames.com for game suggestions based on age ratings to play safely together.
- Geocaching, the world's largest treasure hunt that uses GPS coordinates and is totally free. There will be something near you, and it's also fun to play on holiday. Go to geocaching.com or download the app.
- Make a stop-motion animation. The Stop Motion Maker app is free and costs 99p to remove all ads.
- Film a 'talent show' to share with family/friends you miss or are far away.

It's important not to be afraid of joining your child online in digital pursuits. Some people think of video games as 'online playgrounds' where children can learn about following rules, building alliances, mediating conflict, developing impulse control and how to communicate well with others to reach a final goal. Multi-player games can definitely offer some of these skills, which are not dissimilar to what children might gain from being in a school playground.

Rather than let your child play on their own with a headset, you can be a safety net and active participant in keeping them safe and having fun. Ask them to teach you how to play the game. In doing so, you're also going to learn how it feels to play the game, and appreciate the real risks and emotions that it sparks that might also affect your children. Playing video games together is about being present, and it offers a wonderful opportunity to learn, teach and protect our children.

We want to have some areas in our home where smartphones are not allowed so we can be together without the pressure of responding to messages. We think bedrooms have to be a smartphone-free area because we know screens can have an impact on sleep. We pledge to keep our phones _____ at bedtime. Where else do you think we should make a 'phone-free zone'?

There are going to be times when we use our phones or let you do something on a screen. We want to make sure you are safe when you go online now and when you get a smartphone one day. Where in our home could we make it a safe haven for screen time? We have some ideas but we want to hear yours too . . .

Some people choose a day of the week or month to go fully 'screen free', which means no smartphones, emails or TV. This might be a nice way of making family memories together for real, not online. What do you think about this idea? Is it something we could try?

This pledge is not just for our family, it's a pledge we want to make with friends/family so we are all united in keeping you safe and making smartphones a useful tool you will have access to one day. Who do you think might like to join us in 'unplugging' once a month and/or could support us with the pledge?

[Read and amend the final section of the pledge and sign when you are ready.]

When you write up the Family Phone Pledge, look at each section and choose what to focus on. You don't have to complete all the sections the first time you do it or even involve your children in all of it. You can make some of the rules as parents and choose to invite your children to negotiate some aspects of it, such as identifying which communal areas should be assigned for screen time and where your phones should live when you're at home. You might want to trial some of these things for a week or two as mini experiments to see how they work for your family. You can invite friends to join the Family Phone Pledge and discuss together what works, what doesn't, and generally things to try out. Over the space of weeks, months and, eventually, years, you'll embed healthy habits around smartphones that translate into behaviours you'll see in your child when they get their own. Even if it's not yet, when the time comes the effects will be dramatic.

Reviewing and renegotiating the pledge

The Family Phone Pledge is a 'live' document. It's meant to be adapted in tandem with changes that take place within your family. Whenever you create a plan like this, it's going to be a bit messy and inconsistent, but this is part of the process of behavioural change. Doing 'test trials' of things to see how they suit you as a family is a great idea and shows your children the power of problem-solving, experiencing success and struggles, and making adjustments to get things right. You're likely to hear success stories from friends and family who've also signed up to the pledge and want to give things a try. Go for it! That's the power of the Family Phone Pledge – the sharing of knowledge and ideas between families can support and empower you during the years of smartphone delay. What a rich and interesting time for all of us as families doing this together.

The pledge isn't written in stone and it's OK to make changes, as long as you communicate this clearly with your child or children and you're able to agree the new set of rules or limits. My suggestion is that you sit together as a family to review your pledge once a week or once a fortnight, a bit like you might review and update a shopping list, a weekly planner or your work diary. Some things might stay the same and others might need discussion. I find that this conversation works well on a Sunday morning over a lazy breakfast (ours includes pancakes with chocolate spread but you do you . . .). You can look up to the pledge that hangs on the back of your door or clearly on a wall and open the conversation with something like, 'What went well this week with our Family Phone Pledge?' and leave it for someone to speak and fill the space.

In our house it's often our eldest who'll make a comment along the lines of, 'Mummy did well not carrying her phone,' and when we say, 'Anything that didn't go so well?' she'll say something like,

'Daddy read his phone at the table.' My poor husband, she always has praise for me and a learning point for him. Be mindful that this might also be true in your home, and you may need to bring some balance to the conversation so your children learn that mistakes are allowed, no one is failing and you're all working together to keep the pledge going. To carry this example forward, try saying something like, 'Daddy was very good at putting his phone away when we reminded him and he didn't pick it up again. I also forgot my phone the other day and we had to turn the car around, remember? Oops! It's not that easy, this Phone Pledge, is it? But we're all working at it and learning from our mistakes.'

If you can stick your Family Phone Pledge up on a wall or some other place in your home that's easily visible to all of you, it will make you more likely to notice it and initiate conversations about it. Possible locations might be in the kitchen, dining room, lounge, entrance or pinned on the back of a door. Ours is on the back of our dining-room door, which we tend to close when we eat. This makes it visible when we're all sitting at mealtimes and often sparks discussion, whether we're having a 'pledge review' or not.

How to support each other to keep the pledge

We tend to want to do more of what feels good, which is why reprimanding or correcting someone for behaviour they're working to change can become annoying and cause friction. To some, hearing something like, 'Why have you got your phone out again?' or 'Ugh, the pledge we signed is redundant if you don't care' will not just be a sure way to start conflict, it can also be demotivating and lead both adults and children to want to give up. I don't want this to happen; I want you to feel like you can create a pledge that you and your children feel proud of and want to stick at together, because you know the benefits of delaying smartphones and teaching good habits will have a long-lasting impact on all of you. So, I want you to try the following visualisation exercise.

At times when you or others in your home reach for a screen and you're not following the pledge in the way you negotiated it, try to visualise that someone has just blown bubbles into the air. They're light and shimmery and hard to ignore. You really want to pop them! But if you pause, stay still, catch your breath – deep breath in, slow breath out, like you're cooling down a hot drink – the bubbles will eventually find a place to land and 'pop' all by themselves. If you can wait until the 'imaginary bubbles' begin to pop before you open your mouth to speak, you give yourself a chance to offer encouragement, say something layered with positivity or humour, and transform this moment into a learning point, rather than a jab or a nag. The pause will also give the person who's holding their smartphone a gracious moment to stop and think about their behaviour. Without any prompting they might take a different course of action, such as apologising for their behaviour or explaining why reaching for their phone in that particular moment was important, and you can all go back to doing what you were doing before.

I want you to see these little mishaps not as something you need to monitor and catch so as to ensure you're not 'failing', but to see them for what they are: old, familiar habits that show up as part of the natural process of creating new ones. The more you focus on the positive steps you're trying to implement and celebrate each other for giving your best try, the less space the old habits will take up. To guide you, I've created some sample prompts that focus on positivity, encouragement, respect and little doses of humour. Feel free to adapt them into your words as you see fit.

When someone reaches for their smartphone and it looks like whatever's on the screen is more important to them than what's happening in the real world . . .

- 'Did you leave your smartphone on the table? Would you like me to put it in [agreed space] on charge while we eat?'
- 'I know it's hard to resist the buzzing, but I was really enjoying our conversation. Can you "park your phone" for a bit in [the agreed space] so we can keep talking?'
- 'You want new jeans? There's a lot of choice, and those photos are tiny! You might see them better on the computer. Shall we have a look together once we get home?'

When you forgot that what you were doing isn't visible to others . . .

- 'Sorry, I'm on my phone and you haven't got a clue what I'm doing. How boring! Rosie's on holiday and I was checking how she's getting on. She just sent some photos. Want to see them?'
- 'Nanny just texted and I'm trying to write a reply, but I think it might be easier if I call her. Want to do a video call with me now or a bit later?'

- 'I *am* sorry, I know work should be over, but I've got a deadline and my boss has just messaged me about something. I think it's urgent and I really should sit at a desk and action it now. Can I have fifteen minutes? I'll then put my phone on charge and join you.'

When someone picks up the phone during 'protected non-screen time' . . .

- 'I'm sorry, Uncle Alan, your smartphone isn't invited into this family game of *Dobble*. Please can you put it in [agreed space]? Be quick, we're setting the game up!'
- 'I was really looking forward to watching this film with you. If you need to do something important on your phone, that's OK, I'll wait. When you're done, can you put it in [agreed space] so we can watch this together?'

When you forget something or you get it wrong, don't forget to apologise! This models to your children the behaviour you want to see from them. Show your family that you value their company and interactions, and even if you trip up with the rules, you won't give up.

Just because everyone else is doing something doesn't mean your child has to do it too. Difference is a hard one to accept, and it's a key area that we need to work harder at developing in our children. The same way you might decline the expensive trendy water cup or the lip balm with the £30 price tag, it's OK to say 'not yet' to smartphones.

We tend to think of children as delicate beings who won't be able to tolerate our 'no', and although children do need our empathy and compassion when their wishes and wants are turned down, the truth is that it's us, their loving grown-ups, who struggle to tolerate their distress the most. Children learn resilience in moments of struggle when they're with an adult who cares for their well-being and isn't punishing or shaming them. Your child can sustain a few more years without a smartphone without crumbling or coming to harm, and they'll cope with this more easily when you give them clear expectations, talk through the Family Phone Pledge with a view to listening, include their views and opinions in your joint discussions, invite their friends to join the pledge so no one gets left behind, and make their offline world sufficiently interesting and stimulating.

The Family Phone Pledge is here to help you feel empowered in your decision to delay smartphones and align you with a community of parents that is working towards the same goal: to safeguard children from potential online harms and give us, their parents, a chance to support them in developing offline skills that will allow them to have better digital habits and greater skills to stay safe online. I believe the Family Phone Pledge creates a healthy foundation for smartphones that helps children understand that using them well takes effort, commitment and clearly demarcated boundaries.

I pledge to delay my daughters from smartphone ownership, and I know this needs to come with supervised online experiences that will teach them the discipline and the skills I was never taught to live in harmony with such a powerful piece of digital kit in my pocket. I'd much rather my children go online to explore things in my home with me by their side to teach them coping strategies than know this will happen when they're no longer within the safety of our home. We don't necessarily have to shield our children from all screens or even smartphones completely. We can consider how to introduce digital devices and online experiences in ways that are reasonable, time-limited and safe. It's how we think about our role as parents that's most critical. Remember that one of our jobs is to keep our children safe and that protective boundaries require a certain flexibility as they get older so they can learn how to cope with the challenges that show up with us by their side.

When it comes to digital technology, our children are always on the accelerator pedal, so we should be ready with our foot on the brake. Try not to get frustrated with your children's curious minds, their risk aversion when exploring online and their fascination with the latest technology, video games and apps. Even if they don't have a smartphone, they might see them or hear about all of these in the playground. Meet them in their curiosity, try and explore things online together, and above all, listen to them, understand them and talk. Don't be afraid to say the most obvious simple thing, including, 'I love you, I can't let you have a smartphone yet. I'm sorry waiting is so hard for you. Being a parent is not easy and I promise I'm trying to do my best.' We cannot stop our children from growing up in this digital age, but we can choose how to help them navigate it.

The golden opportunity of having older siblings

The Family Phone Pledge has been designed with whole families in mind, including those with older siblings who might already have a smartphone and younger children who don't. If this is the case for you, I want you to know you're a welcome and important part of the Family Phone Pledge because you come with knowledge, experience and tons of useful lessons you can gift to other parents who, like me, only have younger children and are committing to delay smartphone ownership.

I love elder siblings with smartphones because they can offer a golden opportunity to teach younger children good habits and to share their experiences. As they're not the authority figures that parents are, they have a greater influence when they endorse the rules of the Family Phone Pledge and support the message that waiting for smartphones is a good thing.

Have a conversation with older children to instil in them the important role that they play with their younger siblings. This may sound like, 'Your brother looks up to you and wants to do everything you do. We got you a smartphone when you went to secondary school but looking back, we think it was too soon. We've made the decision to delay getting your brother a smartphone until he's at least thirteen, and we'd really love you to be part of our team to help him with this. We know it's going to be really hard for him to see you with a smartphone, so we need you to follow the rules of the Family Phone Pledge with us.

'It's OK to use your smartphone with your brother around if you want to take photos or a video together, but you're not allowed to post any images or content about your little brother online. He's not allowed to watch social media but if there's something specific you want to show him because it's funny, entertaining or you think he'd like it, come and check with us. If we approve of it, then you can show him too. Does this make sense? Do you have any questions? We'll keep talking about it, and if you make mistakes we'll help you. We're a team now. OK?'

If as a parent you also feel you need to rein in your elder child's smartphone use, I want you to know it's never too late. It always begins with a conversation with your child when you name your worries and concerns, get curious about their behaviour, and finally offer some actions for the next steps you want to take. Make sure you stay objective about what you notice, and own your feelings rather than sharing a judgement.

- **Rather than saying:** 'I think you're addicted to your phone. You can never switch it off at night and you refuse to follow the house rule of keeping it outside your bedroom. We might have no alternative but to take it away if you don't follow the rules.'
- **Try saying something like:** 'I've noticed you struggle to switch off your phone in the evenings and we always end up shouting at each other. I really hate that I feel such dread in the evenings when I have to remind you to bring your phone out of your bedroom. I really want to understand what's happening with you. Why do you find switching off your phone so hard? What can I do to help? Would it work if we agreed you can go to bed thirty minutes later so you have a bit more time with your friends and then switch it off? Do please let me help you.'

You are your children's key source of support. You need to approach challenges with smartphones in a way that brings you closer to your child rather than pushes them away. Children become resistant to talking to us, their parents, when they fear we might confiscate their phones or restrict their social interactions online. This requires us to put in a considerable effort to regulate our emotions, take time to think about how we want to approach dilemmas such as this, and lean into our curiosity to understand our children's teenage worlds online as much as we try and do this offline. By showing your child you're on their side and want to understand their feelings and behaviours better, you position yourself as a much more effective guide who can help them when they really need you.

And if after talking with them you feel the need to implement actions that can help to rein in smartphone use for your older children, here are some ideas to consider and discuss with your child. You can frame them as 'mini experiments' to trial for a week or two to see how it makes things easier or harder. When you suggest ideas like this, remember that change is hard. The first few days might therefore not feel easier, but over time, small shifts might happen whose benefits you and your child can appreciate.

- **Remove the internet browser.** Yes, you can take this off a smartphone and prevent access to the internet.
- **Disable access to the app store.** If you don't already do this, it's a good one to stop your child downloading a million apps and games that are probably distracting their attention from other things.
- **Delete WhatsApp and other social media apps.** This is a hard one for many children, but WhatsApp is available on a desktop, as are Instagram and YouTube. This means you can more carefully supervise your child when they go online via

a computer, limit their social interaction, keep an eye on their behaviour and any 'phone flags' that show up. If it's socialising late into the evening that's a problem, this can set a clearer limit.

- **Try using a mobile phone instead.** If things have become really tricky, or it's early days and you've tried offering your child a smartphone but it has created problems in the relationship you have with them, consider a trial swap with an un-smart mobile phone. These can send and receive text messages and calls, as well as take photos, meaning that your child doesn't have to be completely socially isolated, just protected from some of the things their bodies and minds are saying are too much (review the phone flags in Step 2 to guide you with this).

- **Go retro and set up a family landline.** Who remembers the burger-shaped phone or the translucent one that went neon when it rang? Landlines are so old-school, but many homes still have one for internet access. We have one that sits under the stairs, but I can't tell you what our home landline number is. It's interesting to think about what might happen if we brought landlines back – when people wanted to talk to us, they'd call the landline and our children would learn to chat with their friends too. My in-laws still use their landline, and it's been a consideration of ours for a while.

When you agree a delay on smartphones alongside a clear set of house rules, encourage collaboration with older siblings, have an open dialogue, prioritise family activities (balancing online with screen-based phones), you create a balanced, positive and healthy environment where smartphones are no longer the main focus.

Mobile phone alternatives

I remember when I switched from my bright red flip phone to a smartphone in 2013. I didn't really want to swap; I didn't see the point. I loved my flip phone and I remember hating how big and bulky smartphones were. It didn't make sense to me why I'd need so many things on a phone, or why the screen had to be *so* big, and I think I was one of the last to move on to a smartphone in my friendship group. The thing that clinched it for me? Group texts. I felt left out because I *was* left out! My friends and I once had 'group emails' in which we chatted most days (and yes, this was while I was a working adult in my early thirties). When they all slowly transitioned to smartphones, the email trails stopped and I missed out on the group chat. There was often a 'messenger' who'd kindly relay information back and forth, but obviously this only happened with conversations in which we were trying to arrange a get-together. Otherwise, all the banter and chit-chat was lost on me.

I think it was a useful experience to help me empathise with teenagers who don't have a smartphone. It's *hard*! But now I'm the owner of an iPhone Pro, the largest model they sell. It literally *is* a mini supercomputer that barely fits in my pocket! I mainly use my phone for work and a lot of my communication with my team happens on group WhatsApp. The phone is big so I can see and read things with more ease, and I often think it's absolutely wild that I carry it in my pocket.

Would I personally swap it back to a flip phone? No, I wouldn't. My smartphone helps me work and do things with more ease. *But* – I'm an adult and I'm still learning to put my phone in its place so that it doesn't interfere with the things I want to do in real life. When it comes to children and young teenagers, they don't need 'smartphone intelligence' in their everyday lives. Cinematic-quality video and DSLR-level photographic capability on a mobile device aren't things that children need access to, and we've already talked about social media and unfettered internet access. A smartphone genuinely is a luxury item, and it looks odd and out of place in children's hands.

So if you think it would be sensible, useful or worthwhile for your child to be contactable and be able to message and call their friends, why not consider an alternative to a smartphone? Some people call them brick phones, un-smartphones, dumb phones . . . I think language matters, and children are already going to be put off that they don't look as 'cool' as smartphones or contain anything like the same level of technology, so let's keep it simple and call them what they are – mobile phones. Nokia still do good phones (who remembers playing Snake? Well, it still exists on a Nokia), there are retro flip phones from new brands such as HMD, and mobile phones that have the same style as smartphones but without the internet, such as Pinwheel. You can see and buy most of these phones online via standard phone retailers.

When we delay smartphones but offer children alternatives, we help them learn responsibility and healthy habits around mobile technology. If your child gets a mobile phone the Family Phone

Pledge rules, such as screen-free zones and putting their phone in an agreed location most of the time, apply to them too. Mobile phones are a great way of instilling smartphone skills while limiting the risks. Their need to stay connected with friends outside of school is satisfied, as are the ability to contact you when you're apart and have that little bit of freedom to take photos and videos without leaving a digital footprint on their identity online. If you've never considered these mobile phone alternatives, I urge you to have a look, and if your child is old enough, show them and talk about it with them too. When you pledge to delay smartphones with friends and family, you can also agree to get your children one of these when the time is right. It's win–win.

Step 5
Involving others

One of my friends has three children, with her eldest in Year 6, and she told me about the difficulties of not getting her daughter a smartphone when all her friends already have one. Thoughtfully and under supervision, she agreed to let her daughter use her smartphone to join a group chat with her friends and gave her time after school every evening to do so. But her daughter said that her friends had created a different group chat that she'd been excluded from so they could openly talk about things without her mother spying on them, meaning that her mother's strategy was still making her feel left out. My friend understandably felt overwhelmed and stuck.

This conversation led us to talk about how much time we all spent after school at the age of ten or eleven talking on landlines with our friends, and we laughed at the numerous arguments that this caused in our homes. We talked about how at that time our parents could at least hear half our conversation and thus get the gist of it, and even if they rolled their eyes at us or thought it was utter nonsense, we were by all accounts pretty safe.

Thinking about a child that age in an online group chat with an unlimited number of people made us feel uneasy. Knowing my friend's daughter had been excluded by her friends so her mother couldn't 'spy' on the content of their conversation felt dodgy. Children want and need privacy, but moving to a separate group chat felt like the equivalent of one of us in the 1990s going to a payphone to call our friends after school to avoid our parents overhearing us.

Perhaps we're old-fashioned – indeed, maybe we're just old – but something didn't sit quite right with us about all this, so we agreed to unite around our common concern: delaying smartphones for our children. And now I have my own pledge parenting community.

Don't dismiss out of hand the power of community with other parents. If you're concerned that your child is being left out socially and that there might be a way to get children to spend more time together in the real world, make this happen. Talk to parents, agree social in-person activities on weekends, and ensure your child feels like there are times when they're being allowed to socialise and interact with their friends outside of school without the need for digital technology to take over. If you've agreed to join the Family Phone Pledge together, it's likely these conversations with other families will feel easier. So rather than children feeling like something is being taken away from them, they will understand what the rhythm of life without screens feels like, which makes sticking to the rules a lot easier.

The pledge works best when you join forces with friends and family members, such as the parents of your children's school friends or cousins your children spend time with, and create your own pledge community. I always prefer you to use your own words and include language your children wish to use, like, 'If we have to wait for smartphones, let's do it together!' But just in case it's useful, here are some sample ideas. Change the words, bring your unique essence into it, or copy and paste if you prefer. Whatever works for you – share the pledge and recruit others to join. This is so much easier to do when you're not alone.

As a text message:

Hey, I just read about the Family Phone Pledge, which is about delaying smartphones but with a really useful twist: it helps us build family rules around smartphones and invites us to support each other through the 'smartphone waiting years' not in a virtual WhatsApp, but with regular meet-ups with coffee and snacks. I spoke to [partner's name] and [child's name] and we are IN! Our children love each other and I am really scared that if one of them gets a smartphone the one without will feel excluded and their friendship will get eroded . . . It would be so nice to foster their friendship over the coming years and help each other navigate this and the new stage of smartphone life when we get there . . . What do you think? If you want to learn more let me know. I have a book and a downloadable 'pledge' that is really useful to guide us.

As an email:

Dear [friend's name],

We have decided to not give [child's name] a smartphone until they are [age] and would like to invite you to join the Family Phone Pledge with us.

We know that when children have smartphones it puts them at risk of greater harm from the pull of social media before they have the maturity and coping skills to manage this. We also know that it makes it really hard for any one child to not have a smartphone when all their friends have one because they'll feel excluded from conversations and social activities. When friends don't have a smartphone either, it's a lot easier to wait, because they aren't missing out on anything.

Pledging together gives our children a strong message: that smartphones are not toys created for children, and that it's OK to wait to be a little older to have one in their pocket. We can teach them that smartphones need more maturity and skills too. Our children have agreed to the pledge (can you believe it?) and they were keen for you and your children to come on board too.

The Family Phone Pledge is not just about delaying smartphones, it's also about building a supportive network so we can help each other through the 'smartphone waiting years' and offer each other words of kindness, advice and encouragement. As one of our favourite people, we would love you and your children to join us in this. Parenting is tough and can feel isolating at times. Having to navigate the digital world on top of everything else can feel overwhelming, but together we can make this easier.

We really hope this is something you'd like to join us with. If you want to find out more, let us know. We can share a useful book and a template of the Family Phone Pledge so you can build the rules that feel right for you in your home.

Let me know if you want to chat.

Lots of love,

[name]

By joining up with like-minded parents and engaging parents of children who your children regularly interact with, you'll build a community around the issue of smartphones that will make your Family Phone Pledge and your overall commitment to delaying smartphones more likely to succeed. In fact, studies show that those who belong to a strong community are 76 per cent more likely to achieve their goals, and a supportive community is key to sustained motivation.[1] Supporting each other – ideally face to face – through regular meetings, group chats, coffee mornings or pub lunches to continue to delay smartphones and be a compassionate listening ear, safe sounding board and a source of non-judgemental ideas when dilemmas, struggles and challenges show up can help leverage the positive power of community. This is a human endeavour that needs us to connect with each other in person in real life to make it work for us and our children.

Your pledge, your rules

You've created your unique Family Phone Pledge and are feeling good about it, when – speaking of challenges – your mother-in-law comes round for Sunday lunch and starts scrolling at the table, your newly assigned 'screen-free zone'. Your children give you a questioning look – now what?

If this isn't a situation you've been in before, it's challenging. Who am I kidding, it's challenging no matter how many times you have experienced something like this! In my personal experience, setting boundaries with extended family is the most challenging of all. It's often the older generations who tend to think they have some sort of authority over me that offer the greatest pushback. Understanding the challenges that make it difficult to set boundaries with extended family is an important part of the process of setting respectful, firm limits in your home for yourself and your children.

Sometimes we exaggerate how complicated it's going to be to talk about something, when in reality it can be quite simple. Pre-empting what might happen can help. Openly discuss the Family Phone Pledge before visitors come to your home and clearly but simply state the rules you've agreed. Something like the following might work well:

Hi, we can't wait to see you on Sunday. Please let us know your ETA when you get in the car. We wanted to let you know that we've signed the Family Phone Pledge and have some new rules in our house around smartphones. We have a basket in the kitchen for you to store your phone safely away and get it charged if you need to. It might help to take your phone off silent so you can hear it if it rings. You can use your smartphone on the sofa and in the lounge, but please don't bring it to the dinner table or where the children play. If you have more questions let us know. We can't wait to see you!

Letting visitors know about some of the limits around smartphones you've agreed to follow is like a gentle nudge that says, 'These are our family rules, and the expectations we have of you when we welcome you into our home.' Doing this can help you feel confident in your home, while keeping an open dialogue for people to ask questions or to understand things better if they wish to.

When you clearly state your boundaries and expectations, it makes it more likely that people will choose not to overstep them.

Consistent communication is key, and when setting new rules in your home you've got to accept that offering little reminders might be necessary. You could try something like, 'Sorry, Grandma, no phones allowed at the table. Shall I put it on charge in the kitchen for you? You can pick it up after lunch if you need to.' The more you use language that's respectful and thoughtful while maintaining your boundary, the easier it is for people to follow. You're also modelling language to your children that they can start to use too. So don't be surprised if your child spontaneously says one day, 'I'm sorry, this is a phone-free zone. You can use your phone in the lounge if you like.'

You may be surprised to find that children will engage with the Family Phone Pledge faster and with greater commitment than adults, so use this to your advantage, while still picking them up on vocal tone or inappropriate language if need be. For example, it might come across as brash or rude if your child says, 'Put your phone away!' As you would in other situations, intervene with the intent of teaching your child social skills rather than shaming them; something like, 'Thank you for trying to remind Joanie that we don't use phones when we're playing together. Please can you try again with kinder words?' Or if your child is young or needs a social prompt, suggest that they try: 'Thank you for reminding Joanie to put her phone away. Next time can you say, "Please can you put your phone away? When we play together, we don't like screens to interrupt our fun. Want to have a go?"'

And of course, your in-laws, your parents, friends and any other visitors might not agree with your new home rules around smartphones. They might judge, mock or dismiss the importance of what you're doing either in your presence or once they leave your home, but their views, thoughts and feelings are not yours to control. What you can do is be confident about the decisions you feel are important and healthy for your family. Keep setting high expectations and being a good role model for your children. When you do both of these, you're setting the bar for the value you place on family, relationships, and the amount of space and time you want smartphones to take up.

When your child's friends have smartphones and come into your home

If your child has a friend over, it isn't an overreach of your parental authority to limit their smartphone use when they're guests in your home. I think of this no differently to asking children to take their shoes off when they come into your home or telling them not to play football inside the house. How you communicate your rules is what will probably make the difference, and this may depend on the circumstances.

If a child is coming to your home with their parent for a quick play, you might not have to say anything at all unless a phone or screen appears. If this happens, you might want to communicate your rule about smartphones to the parent you're chatting to with something light that states the limit clearly, such as: 'We don't allow our child to use a smartphone so it would be better if Jess didn't either, if you don't mind?'

If a child is being dropped off at your home for a few hours of playtime or overnight, you might wish to address the issue beforehand by having an open and clear conversation with the parent. Depending on what you feel more comfortable with, you could talk to them face to face and have an open conversation about it or you could send them a text that says something like: 'Hi, We can't wait to see Otis tomorrow. Just so you know, we're limiting screen time and Milo hasn't got access to a smartphone. If Otis wouldn't mind leaving his at home tomorrow, I'd really appreciate it. He can of course use my phone if he needs to text or message you at any time during the playdate.'

If you know that a child has a smartphone for personal or health reasons and they won't willingly leave it behind, you can be respectful of this while maintaining the boundaries in your home. In such a case, a text might sound more like, Hi, We can't wait to see Otis tomorrow. I know he has a smartphone and it's OK for him to bring it. Please remind him that we don't have smartphones at the table or in the bedroom, and that we put them away at these times. I can keep his phone in my room overnight so if it rings/beeps I can take it to him and help him with anything he needs. Hope this is OK? Any problems, do let me know.'

Some parents might actually feel quietly relieved that you're setting rules for their child's smartphone use; others will find it trickier, so it will be worth your while to listen to and understand their point of view. When it's about children coming into your home, your boundaries are important, but respecting others so they feel welcomed and accepted is important too. Don't worry if, after talking to another parent, you come to the conclusion that it makes sense that their child keeps their phone on their person. I imagine that cases such as these will be few and far between, but once in a while it might just happen. If it does, it will provide an opportunity to have a conversation with your child about difference, their friend's unique needs and showing respect, while letting them know that the house rules remain the house rules even when their friend is over. If having friends who use phones or screens in your home becomes challenging for your child, you can discuss and work through this together.

Talking to your child's school

There are ongoing conversations in the UK about banning smartphones in schools. I'm not a big advocate of this, and I'm aware my stance often sparks surprise, even shock. It might sound like it's inconsistent with the views I've shared so far, but it does align with my values as a clinical psychologist who offers evidence-based solutions that are impactful in the long term, not the short term. There's a huge amount of misinformation in the media about smartphones, so it's important to establish what is science and what's just opinion. Otherwise we risk making our feelings dictate the best course of action, and feelings are not facts.

Bans appear to be immediately actionable, and this gives a false sense of safety. Taking something away can often be a stop-gap solution that fails to do what we hope it will do – protect. This is because protection without education and preparation doesn't support children's long-term safety with smartphones or digital technologies. Furthermore, we've got no science to back up claims that a smartphone ban in schools will be effective. A large-scale study of 1,227 children aged twelve to fifteen across thirty schools compared restrictive and permissive policies to smartphone use.[2] Despite the restrictive policies prohibiting phone use during school hours, no associated benefits were found to teenagers' mental health, well-being, physical activity, grade attainment or classroom behaviour.

If this sounds at odds with the idea that phones are distracting, which is supported by reports from young people who state that they interfere with homework and exam revision, it's worth knowing that most teachers wouldn't allow children in class to be scrolling, texting or watching videos in any case. In the same way that they'd pull up a child who was reading a comic in a maths class or tell the two chatterboxes in the corner to stop being disruptive and pay attention, most teachers won't allow children to lose focus for more than a few seconds, and this will be the same whether the object of distraction is a smartphone or not. So even when school policies are permissive and allow children to bring smartphones into school, children will only use them at breaktime and lunchtime, not learning time. Furthermore, it's been found that children in restrictive schools may lock away a 'fake' phone and keep their smartphone on them to use in secret.

Bans tend not to work because young people are smart enough to get around them, and if they do subsequently encounter dangerous or distressing content they'll find it harder to seek help or tell an adult because of the fear of repercussions for going behind adults' backs. As a parent, I also don't think we need a ban. Yes, it might feel like it will make delaying smartphones for your child that much easier, but it won't stop smartphones from existing, nor will it stop children using them outside of school or indeed be any sort of preparation for how to use them well.

Rather than a ban, there are better things schools can do to mitigate the risks of smartphones, and to educate and prepare children for smartphone use. Schools can form part of your community of support and become supporters of the pledge. There's evidence that schools can offer personal, collective and proxy levels of support.[3] The issue is that schools often lack the time, funding and resources to be able to put effective structures of this sort in place, but I believe in the power we have as parents to enact changes in our communities. So, if you feel strongly pulled to do so, you might want to write an email or letter to your school enquiring about the level of education they offer children on smartphones and whether there are any ways in which they can support the pledge. I've drafted something you might like to send to your school or adapt in your own words. I'd suggest that signing this with a number of parents who are part of the pledge and would like to discuss these issues with your school will be more empowering and carry more weight than simply sending it on your own.

Dear [headteacher]

We're a group of parents who have pledged to delay smartphones for our children until the age of at least thirteen and would like to discuss ways in which you and our school can support all children in remaining protected and prepared for using smartphones one day.

Our children are born digital natives but don't have digital skills, which must be taught. Science tells us that it's in these early years that we have the greatest opportunity to support our children in learning skills that will protect them from falling into the traps social media lays out for them, that they must learn to develop social skills and emotional skills in the real world in order to use them well online, and that becoming safe online is as big a priority as teaching them phonics, correct grammar or biology. We think school is key in supporting our children build relevant skills, and only a few tweaks might be necessary to make this possible. Here are some ideas.

We'd much appreciate school offering teaching on how to make informed decisions online such as how to spot or avoid disinformation, awareness of AI tricks and AI design, and strategies to reduce digital distractions.

As part of relationships, sex and health education (RSHE), a welcome addition would be to focus on digital world relationships and interactions, including what being a 'good online citizen' looks like, how to spot and stand up to cyberbullying, what digital consent means, and developing skills to manage big feelings that might show up when socialising online, such as using techniques from cognitive behavioural therapy (CBT) to challenge thoughts when friends don't respond to 'read' messages, and teaching children how to navigate these scenarios in the real world when they see each other at school the following day.

We've read about the value of 'peer-to-peer' learning approaches where children can work together. These include teaching and encouraging children to form pacts to consent to sharing photos of each other before tagging or posting, and doing this as a whole classroom exercise so children are accountable to each other, offering peer support and peer protection too.

We also wonder whether you've ever considered inviting children to share their views on smartphones. Children's voices are often not heard, and it might be useful to consider partnering with them to co-write the school policy on smartphone use at school based on their opinions and views.

All the above ideas are evidence-based and have already been trialled in schools. If you'd like some further reading, please let us know and we would be happy to share.

We hope that as part of the school curriculum you might be willing to include some of these ideas. Please let us know when we can meet with you to discuss this further.

We look forward to hearing from you and continuing to work together.

Best wishes,

Pledge signatories [no. of parents]

Altogether, this is about building a safe 'ecosystem' at school and embedding an ethos of how to use smartphones well before children have access to them. To me, this feels like an important aspect of education that schools should get involved with. These ideas are more pressing and impactful in our current society than learning times tables by rote. It's time our children's formal education reflected our modern society, and getting involved in this conversation should feel pertinent to schools rather than a burden.

How to navigate peer relationships around smartphones outside your home

If you're reading this book while your children are at primary school, I sincerely hope that by the time they're teenagers it will no longer be the norm to have a phone at the age of eleven. This will hopefully make redundant the question of how to prepare your child for navigating peer relationships outside of your home when their friends have smartphones and they don't. That said, the current norm of 'smartphones by eleven' might still be in place, so let's talk about it. If you've managed to empower friends to sign the pledge with you, it might be a good starting point to discuss the things I raise below together and find mutual support through this when the time comes.

Our generation of children were born with digital devices all around them. Socialising online with friends is not just the norm for young people, it's integral to how they interact with friends. This might feel odd or wrong to you as a parent, particularly if it wasn't something you grew up with. Rather than fear this, however, understanding it and finding ways to prepare yourself and your child while you delay smartphones is key. The Pew Research Center carried out a national survey on teens, technology and friendships in which they found that 95 per cent of teenagers spent time in person with friends outside of school on a regular basis, albeit not as an everyday occurrence, while 55 per cent of teenagers text-messaged their friends daily.[4] Of these, the majority (27 per cent) used instant messaging apps, 23 per cent used social media and 5 per cent used video calls. If we think about this within the context of adolescence, a critical time during which socialising with peers is a vital stage for healthy identity development and individuation,[5] it makes sense that teenagers are using online technologies to socialise and stay connected.

Although we know that text messaging isn't the most meaningful type of contact we can have with others, it's quick, easy and meets the needs of teenagers to have that instant sense of connection. Even while you delay the ownership of smartphones, you can offer your child opportunities to stay connected to peers by using instant messaging apps; either allow your child to borrow your phone (for a time-limited period) or download the app onto your laptop and let your child use it in a safe, communal, 'screen-friendly' area in your home. This may meet your child's need to stay in touch with friends and feel part of conversations, while keeping at bay for the time being the 'everywhere, all the time' nature of smartphones.

When it comes to breaktime at school and some of your child's friends take their smartphones out, you can prepare your child by letting them know this might happen – 'When you're at school I know you might see Lexi take out her phone.' But you have to separate the decision of buying or not buying a smartphone (which lies with us, the adults, and is our right to choose), with how your child might feel at breaktime with their peers (which is absolutely their right to feel). Rather than try and encourage your child to tell their friends to 'come off your phone, let's chat!' or do something else, give your child a choice of what they can do at breaktime. And if you want your child to trust you and tell you truthfully what they've been up to, give them permission to live vicariously through their friends' phone at breaktime.

You might say something like, 'Lexi is your friend, and I get that you'll want to spend time with her at breaktime. If she's on her phone, you can ask her to show you what she's doing, or if it's no fun to do that, you can invite her to do something else with you. You know you won't get a smartphone until you're at least thirteen, but you'll never get into trouble for watching or seeing things on your friends' phones at school.'

Use this as an opportunity to practise having an open dialogue about the online world: ask what Lexi likes to do on her phone at breaktime – does she watch videos, chat to friends (who? Are they in the same school?), play games? What's it like for your child to watch these things? This can all be useful information for you and your child to get an idea of what it might be like when they have a smartphone, the things they look forward to doing and maybe the things they've already learnt they don't want to do when the day comes. Trust that your children can make good decisions for themselves and guide them to use their critical-thinking skills. Experiencing smartphones from a distance can help to open up reflections about what's enjoyable for them, what they find useful and what might be risky.

As your child gets older it can feel hard to relinquish control, but this is a core part of parenting: you work hard to instil certain values and skills so you can send them off into the world to be their own person. My greatest hope is that all the work you've done up to this point will mean that when your children face challenges, they'll be prepared to overcome them and seek support appropriately. Importantly, they'll still have you, their loving adult, to hold them, offer them reassurance and guide them through. It's the best any of us can do, and if you have reached this far, I've no doubt you've done more than enough for all of this to be true.

Involving others to join the pledge or support you with it, as well as navigating the challenges that come up, can feel like a lot of hard work. I've tried to simplify this for you, but it can become time-consuming. Start with the people in your community who matter the most to you, and see how your courage and skill at involving others grows from there. Protecting and preparing our children to live with smartphones is everyone's business. When it comes to children, all adults are accountable for looking out for children's well-being within a society, and building a community around yourself to help give you support with this is part of your due diligence.

Step 6

Find your SPARK

Now that you're committed to change and embedding new, healthier habits with your smartphone, let's get into the nitty gritty of 'what' this might look like. If you try to change *all* of the initial things in your Family Phone Pledge at once – how you use your phone, the amount of time you spend on it and what you do with it – it can be overwhelming. That's why I have simplified these actions for you in five areas that I've called SPARK. This stands for:

S = Socialise

P = Presence

A = Access

R = Rest and sleep

K = Knowledge

For each letter in the acronym, I'll describe what you need to bring your awareness and attention to, and offer a set of toolkits to guide you. Take what's useful to you and leave the rest. Some strategies might work well in the first weeks of living according to your pledge, whereas others might be more useful later on, so feel free to revisit this section when challenges crop up. I hope you find the 'little tweaks' that can have a positive influence on how you and your family feel and think around your smartphones and the pledge you've just signed.

Socialise

Prioritise real-life connections

When you start building better habits with your phone, it's a good thing to try to spend a greater amount of quality time with friends and family. You might send out text messages every day, but when was the last time you met those friends you text? And what about the people who like and comment on your family photos on social media? When was the last time you shared a drink with them in real life?

There are going to be people who are far away from you that you don't or can't see on a regular basis. There are a lot of people in my social circle whom I don't see on a yearly basis. I moved to the UK from abroad and have friends scattered across most continents around the world. This is also true for my family. But the way we navigate this is to have semi-regular meet-ups via group video calls. It's something we started during the Covid-19 lockdowns, and it felt very connecting and actually joyful to see friends' faces and hear their voices, even – especially – from the other side of the world. And it's something we have continued to do because it feels good.

If you're going to use a smartphone, video calls are the most meaningful way to connect with others and will bring some feel-good hormones. When you don't want to or can't show your face, a phone call or a voicenote is far better than just sending a text. But don't forget to protect time to see them in real life, without your phone, to foster closeness and have meaningful conversations. It's so important for our children to see that our smartphones are not the things that connect us, they're simply tools we use to help us meet up with others face to face and create real-life memories.

Snap out of becoming a 'smartphone zombie'

Most people use their phones in silence. Your brain might be working hard and what you're doing is probably not mindless, but to those around you, while you stare into your screen ignoring them and the world around you, you look like a 'smartphone zombie'. Changing this is quite simple to do. As we've discussed, sharing what you're doing or are about to do on your phone can connect your smartphone actions with the people who surround you in the real world, and this will make you more human.

If you're using your phone to do your weekly supermarket shopping from home, you might say, 'I need to add lemons to our food order before I forget'; if it's a social thing, it could be something like, 'I didn't reply to my friend's message earlier. I'm going to do it right now.' It can help you to stay accountable to each other when you've agreed to try this action but don't follow through, so if your child's other parent opens the door to the online world without graciously sharing what they're doing, ask, 'What's going on? You're reading something with a lot of focus,' or simply, 'What are you doing on your phone?'

As you and your family become accustomed to sharing what you get up to on your phones, you'll become increasingly aware of your behaviour. For example, I've learnt that my husband doesn't use his phone for socialising. It's mainly a tool to 'do' things, like buy new items, read the news or set up calendar alerts. For me, on the other hand, 90 per cent of the time it's to socialise with friends and the rest is spent on social media. It's interesting to learn how we use our phones differently and that for the most part we're not 'wasting time', but every now and then being on our phone can wait for a better moment. Sharing what you do on yours invites you to question, 'Do I need to do this, right now?' That tiny reflection can make all the difference.

Presence

Let go of your phone

How often do you switch off your phone completely? I bet these times are vanishingly rare. Perhaps when you're on a flight, and maybe at the cinema, theatre or other public event where interruptions aren't appreciated. Where else would you choose to completely switch your phone off? In all honesty, I couldn't think of any other times when I would have switched off my phone before I started on the epic task of writing this book. I hadn't realised that I'd unconsciously given my phone a home on my person and in my pockets. I realised I needed to find my phone a new 'home', somewhere it could be parked and left to recharge, which is why I included space for you in the pledge template to decide where your smartphones go when they're not in use. A phone isn't a living thing that needs my company. It's an electronic object I don't have to carry around with me everywhere, all the time.

We're more likely to check our phones when they're on our person. This is a bad habit they've trained us to do very well, with their constant buzzing and alerts. But when you find somewhere to put your phone and it's no longer physically in your presence, a distance is created that makes it far easier not to reach out for it unless you've got a clear purpose in mind. Think about what this might look like for you, set it up and do it!

Turn off notifications

The thing that's going to disrupt your social interactions with others more than anything else is the incessant buzzing and pinging of notifications. These persistent alerts are like a needy toddler whining for our attention, constantly and repeatedly. But rather than get annoyed and try to make our phones stop nagging us by turning off notifications, we tend to reach out and respond. If you find that this gets in the way of meaningfully being with people, it's not surprising, but you can do something about it.

The fastest, easiest way to shut off all notifications is to do a 'notification detox'. If you have never done this, it's simple. Go to your phone settings, click on notifications, then scroll and switch them off for each app in turn. Unfortunately, there's no shortcut – you've got to do it one by one. Yes, it's time-consuming, but it's going to teach you a valuable lesson: there are tons of apps on your phone that you don't need and you can painlessly get rid of. It's actually quite liberating to simplify and declutter your phone screen. Give it a try!

This will have an instant effect – your phone has now become a soundless box. You're probably going to reach out for it just out of habit to check if any messages have popped up, but don't judge yourself for doing this. If you keep notifications switched off for a week, you'll soon notice that you stop looking at your phone mindlessly and instead do so with a sense of purpose. Think about it. Which apps do you check the most? Which do you miss getting a notification from? Which ones become easily forgotten?

I found the lack of buzzing on my person and in my home a welcome silence I'd missed but forgotten all about. I still needed to hear calls, messages and some notifications that are important, but now I don't carry my phone around with me at home at all times, so I had to do something better than looking in the basket to check messages at random. The simple answer: put the ring tone back on, rather than keep it on silent.

Do you remember *Trigger Happy TV*, the hidden-camera TV show with Dom Joly? The loud ring tone of a Nokia would sound (just typing that out makes me hear it), and Dom would pick up a giant mobile phone and shout 'HELLO! I can't talk, I'm on a pedalo!' (or in the library, an art gallery or restaurant). If you haven't seen it, you can find it online and it's worth a watch – it's still hilarious. This satirical take on the early days of mobile phone culture provided an important message about the irritation of mobile phones interrupting everyday life.

The problem is that smartphones are now interrupting us silently and sneakily, shifting our attention from the present moment, becoming a chronic stressor at times. I want to bring back the ring tone, maybe not for all public spaces but for when you step into your home and take your phone out of your pocket. Find a ring tone you like, switch it to loud and let go of your phone. Whenever it rings – and hopefully it won't be often, because you've turned off all of those unnecessary alerts – it will be a bit like a phone doorbell signalling that someone wants to say something to you. You now have the freedom to open that door or let whoever's ringing leave a message you can pick up later.

Access

A section of your pledge focuses on agreed safe sites your child is allowed to visit. Although you're an adult, this also applies to you. You have a responsibility to model what safe and healthy online access looks like, so your child is more willing to follow the pledge alongside you.

You probably access the internet and online world daily, if not hourly, but have you ever been taught the skills you need to stay safe online? Do you know what steps to take to safeguard your personal data and keep you protected from scams, fraud or the very real risk of ending up in a doomscroll session? I wish adult digital literacy was something our society valued and was willing to offer in all workspaces. Most of us don't possess the skills to stay safe within the online worlds we inhabit, so how are we going to support our children in this endeavour? It's not within my remit to offer you a comprehensive guide for this, but I do want you to think about your digital diet, what you consume and how you stay safe when you're online. So here's a small toolkit of ideas to help you. If you already do all of these, you're in a minority, but why not pass these ideas on to someone you know or an extended family member? Older generations struggle in this regard even more than we do, and are at greater risk.

Use strong passwords

You must protect your emails and online accounts well with strong passwords.

If you use the same password for everything, it makes it very easy for cyber criminals to hack all your accounts and access all your information, including bank details. They can also contact others and pretend to be you, reset all your passwords to block your access to websites, and in some instances use this information to blackmail you. Ideally, you should use strong, unique passwords for each of your online accounts and when you can, set up two-step verification, which offers an additional layer of security.

One of the ways to come up with a password that's difficult to crack is by combining three random words separated with hyphens or full-stops (e.g. unicorn-rainbows-glitter or football. chocolate.playstation). Teach your child how to set strong passwords and not share them with anyone (with the exception of other members of your family, as per the Family Phone Pledge's open password policy), to not write them at the front of their school book and not to type them out in front of others. Show them how you use passwords when you open emails and who has access to them.

If you need help remembering your passwords like I do, don't write them down on a piece of paper or on a message stored in your smartphone. Use a password manager instead (I use the Passwords app) or save them to your computer browser.

Update your devices

I wish I could see a show of hands for how many of you regularly update your devices, or even better, set up the automatic update function. Updates are not just nice to have, they keep your data and devices safe. They often include protection from viruses and other kinds of malware, improvements to the software that remove annoying or even critical glitches, as well as introducing new features. If you haven't done this in a while – or ever? – I urge you to do so. Please don't ignore the prompt to update your device. It's one of the most important and quickest things you can do to keep yourself safe online (and it's an easy safety tip to teach your child too).

Pay attention to the algorithm

We all know that algorithms curate our online experiences, so I'd like you to do a little experiment with me. Log on to one of your social media apps – if you have one – and head to the 'Explore' section (on Instagram, for example, it's the magnifying lens icon at the bottom of the screen). Now have a scroll – what do you see? It 'should' look like videos and posts on topics you've either searched for, commented on or shown interest in online. If what you see shocks you, upsets you or makes you feel embarrassed, it might be time to think about the content you choose to view online because the algorithm didn't come up with these suggestions at random.

At the end of the day, algorithms are simply tools that make tech companies money. They need us to stay engaged with content because when we do, they can share more ads and collect more data on our activity online. What you like, share, comment on and even how long you spend online helps algorithms predict the sort of content you find most interesting, and they can manipulate this to show you more of what gets you hooked next time.

Different platforms use algorithms in their own way:

- Facebook prioritises posts from friends, family and long comments.
- Instagram focuses on recent posts with high engagement and most shares.
- X posts retweets and comments but doesn't care about likes.
- TikTok predominantly focuses on watch time.

Understanding algorithms is important because they can distort our online experience. When you only see content that reinforces your views, such as looking solely at parenting platforms, which all share similar messages, you end up in an online echo chamber that strengthens your biases and creates the illusion that everyone thinks like you do. In real life this would be the equivalent of only ever meeting parents who feed their children exactly the same range of foods that you do. This might feel comforting at first, but you'd be missing out on all sorts of options, ideas and differences that might be healthy for you and your children too.

Paradoxically, negative content often traps people into staying engaged online because of its shock factor. You can inadvertently end up in a bad-news loop, seeing content that's distressing or harmful. When children and teens go online, this is more likely because they're more vulnerable to this type of content. They don't swipe past; they watch even if it's in horror.

Algorithms shape what you see online and what you miss out on. Taking back control is important, and you can do this by understanding how they work and choosing to take helpful actions, including:

- Be selective about what you like, share and comment on. This shapes the online content you get shown.
- Interact with sources of information you trust, which will lead to more high-quality information, and avoid those you don't. I often get sent links to videos and refuse to watch them if they come from sources that look in any way dodgy. Protecting the content I view is important to me.
- Actively seek out different voices and perspectives. For example, look out for content online about the benefits of video games or how social media can create communities of support. You can choose to delay smartphones *and* keep an open mind.
- Take control of your settings. Turn off ads with an ad blocker, keep personal information private and limit tracking (look at the settings on your apps for this).

Rest and sleep

If you and your family commit to your Family Phone Pledge and implement all the boundaries it contains, I guarantee you'll find your rest and sleep improve. It's worth highlighting here why both are important and how to prioritise them. As we talked about earlier in the book (see page 71), the research we have on sleep shows that good sleep is fundamental to well-being. One night of sleep deprivation, or less than five hours' sleep, can lead to a 60 per cent increase in reactivity in the amygdala.[6] In other words, if you don't manage to get those five hours, your response to stress is likely to be worse, you'll be more irritable and will struggle to interpret other people's emotional states. We know that without sufficient REM sleep, the brain struggles to distinguish between real threats and non-threatening situations, which can make our stress and fear responses more exaggerated.

In a nutshell, if you're sleep deprived you'll struggle to function effectively. This is true for us, the parents who are inevitably sleep deprived, and it's true for our children too. So what can you do? My advice is to focus on rest. As a parent you might well be sleep deprived for a few years to come, and while you might not think that parents can rest much either, there are ways of resting that you'll find both doable and nourishing.

Learn to rest, and do it every day

Most people have the idea that to 'rest' means having a nap or doing nothing at all, both of which are borderline impossible for most people who juggle work and parenting. But rest can be so much more than that. It's about finding ways that help you be present more meaningfully in the spaces and with the people you want to be. The type of rest that works for you will be influenced by your personality, as well as the context you're in.

The psychology of rest focuses on understanding the role of rest in mental and emotional well-being.[7] Take a look at these seven types of rest and consider which are most important to you, and which you might want to bring into your life more regularly:

1. **Emotional rest: time away** – this might be time away from people, or simply taking a holiday, but it can also mean doing something just for fun. As adults we often lose the skill of playfulness, but when we engage in it we can be emotionally recharged and energised. Think of things that you enjoy, make you laugh or bring out your silly side, then put some time aside to schedule these in (as well as booking a holiday to look forward to!).

2. **Spiritual rest: permission to not be helpful** – as a parent, you most likely pour all your time and energy onto your children, your home and even your spouse (if you have one). But taking care of others takes energy, and if you're going to keep going, you need to find deep rest. Make it a priority to pay attention to your own needs and take a break from being helpful. Pass some of your responsibilities on to someone else, or skip the children's bathtime every now and again so you have some extra 'me' time in the evening.

3. **Sensory rest: take a 'duvet day'** – In a world full of constant stimulation it's important to protect times to reduce this overload. This might look like booking a day where you unplug your smartphone and 'unschedule' everything. From the moment you wake up in the morning, you can engage in activities that you want to do rather than focusing solely on

what you need to do. This can help you get more focused and feel calmer too.

4. **Creative rest: connect with nature and/or art** – as human beings we derive much of our well-being from spending time in nature and/or connecting with our more creative side. Rest can come from a walk through the woods, walking barefoot on the grass for a few minutes to ground yourself or even doing some mindful colouring or drawing. When our brains focus on nature or art, they offer us a mindful break from the busyness of life.

5. **Mental rest: time to recharge** – for some people, rest comes with alone time. This might be something like going to the cinema on your own, eating in a café by yourself or just doing the shopping alone. When you've got limited energy to offer, protecting time to be free of others' demands and just focus on yourself can feel deeply restful.

6. **Physical rest: take a nap** – power naps can be as short as twenty minutes and help you feel a lot better in order to keep going with your day. Rather than scroll on the sofa for half an hour, set a timer, get an eye mask, rest your head on the pillow and . . . snooze. Your body and mind will thank you.

7. **Social rest: quality time with friends** – when you spend time with people who you feel safe with and make you feel seen and heard, it can allow your body and mind to decompress and find some rest. Book time for meaningful friendships and try to distance yourself from relationships that are draining or stressful. This might be hard to do but it can help you feel more fulfilled in your relationships and improve your mood

too. Rest is not just a physical necessity – it's also crucial for our minds and emotions. Make sure to plan 'rest snacks' across your day or at a minimum across your week, and your mind and body will thank you.

Ban smartphones and all screens from bedrooms

I mentioned earlier that it's not the light that smartphones emit but the way screens engage and hold our attention that has the greatest impact on sleep. Smartphones keep us wanting to watch and message more, which means our brains stay awake for longer. In our home we've had one rule from day one (even before having children): there are no screens in bedrooms. Your pledge will specify where your phone should be when not in use and demarcate screen-free zones in your home.

One of these zones that's good to commit to is bedrooms. As someone who loves sleep (probably more than crisps, and that's saying a lot), I've always protected bedrooms as sanctuaries for rest and sleep. Nowadays our children's bedrooms are filled with toys, and my eldest sometimes chooses to play in her bedroom with her friends, away from her little sister's mischief, but bedrooms are still not the place for physical, energetic play, and the bed is not used for anything other than resting, reading or sleeping.

An important caveat is that some science suggests that neurodivergent children, such as those who are autistic or have ADHD, find engaging with screens soothing in an otherwise overwhelming and unpredictable world.[8] They might therefore benefit from some screen time before bed as a way to wind down. If this works for your child, there's no need to make any changes, and there may be some little tweaks you can make to improve their sleep hygiene.

It's worth knowing that sleep hygiene begins in the day, and considering what you eat and drink, how much you move your body and what your bedroom environment is like is key.

Daytime tips

- **Get sunlight soon after waking.** Seeing sunlight – or any bright light – shortly after waking up lets your brain know it's time to slow its melatonin production and start getting ready for daytime. If you live in a place that doesn't get much sunlight, consider giving your child a bright lamp to turn on after waking up.
- **Limit or avoid caffeine.** Caffeine is a stimulant that prevents sleep and is present in tea and coffee, as well as energy drinks and many fizzy pop drinks. Children are being marketed energy drinks that give 'a physical and mental boost', and many reports show that over a third of children between the ages of thirteen and sixteen are consuming an energy drink at least once a week.[9] Energy drinks lead to poor sleep, raised blood pressure, irritability, anger, poor school performance, anxiety, stress and suicidal thoughts. Since 2024, many retailers have introduced a voluntary ban on selling energy drinks to under-sixteens, but this isn't enforced by law.
- **Move your body.** We know that a sedentary lifestyle will make falling asleep harder. Make sure you move your body:

'walk and talk' when you get a phone call, create time for some exercise, or throw a mini disco in the kitchen while you make dinner and invite your children to move their bodies too.

- **Eat earlier.** When our child started school, we moved dinnertime from 6 p.m. to 5 p.m. Although this is incredibly early for someone like me, who grew up having dinner closer to 9 p.m., and some might find it difficult to implement around standard working hours, it works better for all of us. Eating a big meal can prevent sleep. Children often feel hungrier after school, meaning that they're more likely to eat better earlier in the evening, and once the digestive juices have started, they'll sleep better as a consequence too (this is also true for you!).

Bedtime tips

- **Create a 'sleepy routine'.** Choose two or three items from the following list: taking a warm bath or shower, brushing teeth, putting on pyjamas, having a gentle massage with moisturiser, listening to relaxing music, having a warm drink, occupying yourself with a quiet activity such as a puzzle or a crossword, doing some stretching, practising breathwork, reading a book. Many children find water stimulating, so washing in the morning to perk them up might work better. Some children prefer to chat before they fall asleep, but try to set a clear boundary for when the conversation ends and settling down for sleep begins (e.g. 'I love talking to you, but I've set a timer for five minutes. When it rings, we'll switch off the lights because it's bedtime'). Try as far as possible to keep the routine consistent, while accepting that it might change both as your child gets older and during holidays.

- **Dim the lights thirty minutes before bedtime.** Try dimming the lights in the evening before the bedtime routine starts. If your child uses a screen to unwind, make sure it's stored outside their bedroom and use the dimming of the lights as a signal for bedtime.

- **Aim for a regular sleep schedule.** Setting a time to rise and go to sleep every day helps to ground our circadian rhythm. Children are more sensitive to this, so it can help to stick to within one hour of the usual times on weekends and holidays too, although you should allow a bit of a buffer to decrease the pressure on yourself and your child. For example, if you set bedtime as 7.30 p.m. and notice your child doesn't tend to fall asleep until 8 p.m., don't push it. Instead, move bedtime to be somewhere between 7.45 p.m. and 8.15 p.m. so you and your child can feel successful.

- **Keep the bedroom cool, dark and quiet.** If there's noise or light that can't be avoided, try offering your child a sleep mask and use a white noise machine to muffle intrusive sounds.

- **Plan for enough time in bed.** Children of primary school age need between nine and twelve hours of sleep per night on average, while teenagers need around eight to thirteen. Teenagers are likely not to be ready to fall asleep until later, around 11 to 11.30 p.m. due to a sleep shift caused by hormonal changes. This also means that in the morning they're likely to want to sleep in. Allow them to do this when possible, such as at weekends.

- **If it's not working, get out of bed.** If you're still wide awake after lying in bed for thirty minutes, or feeling anxious or frustrated, getting out of bed is actually a good idea. The bed is a place to feel relaxed and sleepy, not somewhere to toss and turn. If your child gets out of bed, don't raise your voice at them. Instead, help them do something relaxing or boring that invites sleepiness in. Try to pick an activity from your sleep routine and do it in dimmed lighting before taking them back to bed.

If sleep hygiene is new to you, choose one or two of the above to begin with and include more once these become a habit. Overwhelming children with change can cause stress and makes it more likely that you'll give up. Accept that embedding changes – and this applies to all of those you've included in your pledge – takes time, so try to do things gradually. Removing screens can help set the scene for sleep, but screens are not the only things that can inhibit sleep. Focus on a holistic approach to sleep and model this to your child to embed healthy habits for life.

Knowledge

As parents, we need to build skills to impart knowledge to our children in most areas of life. This includes things like emotions, social norms, support with academic skills, relationship skills and personal hygiene, to name but a few. There are topics and content our children might be exposed to online that we need to know and get comfortable talking about because, eventually, they'll get a smartphone and encounter them, if they've not done so already. I won't go into these topics in great detail, but I do want to offer some scripts and toolkits to guide you as they're not generally covered in the school curriculum. This means that the only place your child will hear about them is through you. I know there are other things your child might face online, but I've chosen three areas of concern that parents often share with me: porn, body image and bullying. For all of them the following tips are useful to hold in mind.

- It's never too late to talk. If you've avoided some of these topics in the past, you can choose to engage with them now.
- Before you talk, think about what will help you stay calm: take deep breaths, drink some water, get comfortable, and create a relaxing and private space in which to talk. Tell yourself, 'Talking will help protect my child.'
- Don't sit your child down for a chat. This can feel staged and might be awkward for them. Initiate it as naturally as possible, such as when driving in the car, walking the dog or making dinner together.
- Keep the tone of the conversation casual and open, rather than one-sided. You want to send your child the message that they can talk to you about any topic and you're interested in their thoughts.
- Recognise that this isn't a one-off chat. It's a conversation that you'll have many times. It's OK to get it wrong; if you say the wrong things, just try again at a later stage.

- Remember, there's never a perfect time to talk. The worst conversation on these topics is having no conversation at all. So just do it. I know you can.

The porn conversation

Free online porn is easily accessible on the internet and you'll find it wherever you can access content for free. It's not confined to adult sites; many online platforms such as Reddit and X contain pornographic content.

Put simply, porn is made-up sexual stories created to look real. Online free porn is often violently misogynistic, and leaves people of all ages, genders and sexual orientations with a misunderstanding of what sex and respectful relationships are. When we talk to our children about this topic, it's important to share some of the facts and what your limits are, while leaving space in the conversation for dialogue. You might say something like:

I want to talk to you about a subject that no one ever talked to me about. When I say the word 'porn', what do you think it is?

I know you might see porn at some point, as it's practically unavoidable online!

Porn is images or videos of make-believe sex. It's often created like a story where there's nudity, sexual acts between people and sometimes the use of objects too. Porn often looks real but it's fake. People who make porn often use artificial body parts, filters and make-up to make bodies look different, and sexual scenes are acted out that would never happen in real life.

I know this is super-awkward – no one wants to talk about porn with their parents – but my job is to keep you safe. Porn isn't bad, but free porn can be harmful and watching too much of it can mean you expect relationships and sex to look and feel like porn does. Real sex is not like this. Sex is consensual, people allow each other to touch their bodies because they want to. It's more than just saying 'yes' or expecting someone to get naked for you. It is about telling someone what feels good with their body and what does not, and it's about respect. If someone wants to stop, no matter how into it you are, the right thing to do is to stop. No one should ever make you feel bad, guilty or pressured into doing something you don't want to do, and you should never pressure anyone to do anything they don't want to do with their body.

If you ever see porn, either accidentally or through a pop-up or because you searched for something out of curiosity, I want you to know that you won't be in trouble and you can come and talk to me. I'm always here for you.

A government-commissioned review between 2021 and 2022 found that by the age of nine, 10 per cent of children had seen porn online, 27 per cent had seen it by the age of eleven and 79 per cent had encountered violent pornography by the age of thirteen.[10] Although talking about this topic might feel tricky, it's important not to avoid it and to have age-appropriate conversations. Ensure you start conversations about puberty early, using books to help you, and allow your child to ask questions.

Some girls start menstruating at around the age of nine, so beginning some of these conversations at around age seven can make discussing more complex topics such as sex and porn easier. Talk about the things that go into making relationships healthy and how they should listen to their gut when things don't feel right. Explain what consent means, how to respect boundaries, and what is and isn't appropriate when it comes to touching others. My first book has a useful chapter on all of this, with scripts and tools to guide you.[11]

The body-image conversation

Body dissatisfaction has been linked to risk-taking behaviours and poor mental health. In a recent survey, 36 per cent of teenagers reported they'd do 'whatever it takes' to look good, with 57 per cent considering going on a diet, 10 per cent contemplating cosmetic surgery and, among boys, 10 per cent thinking about taking steroids to achieve their goals.[12]

In the current online climate where we're constantly exposed to unrealistic body standards, it's unsurprising that young people have poor body image. Social media also encourages more negative comparisons with others based on appearance, be it their bodies, their pristine cream-coloured homes devoid of toys and clutter or their perfectly curated holiday photos, miraculously free of tantrums and chaos. Online photos and videos are frequently heavily edited, with lighting, make-up and other effects used to enhance and falsify reality. None of us can easily escape making comparisons and feeling deflated, and it's important to reflect on how going online leaves you feeling too.

Children often take selfies or create videos with friends on their smartphones. When children constantly check their appearance, it can lead to unhealthy comparisons, create unrealistic expectations and put pressure on them to try to create 'perfect' images. Thoughts about body image can begin with 'I hate my thighs,' which can become 'I hate my body' and on some occasions turn into 'I hate myself.' These negative thoughts are often ones we have too, and it's worth recognising how we speak about our bodies and the comments we make about others. We play a critical role in supporting our children to develop critical thinking around the images they see online, and it's helpful to look at images together and keep the conversation open. You might say something like:

Bodies come in all shapes and sizes. It's hard not to compare yourself to others, but I want you to remember that there's only one you. Tell me what you love about your body and what you'd like to be different? What would you change if you could? How would that make you feel? How do you think it would change the person you are?

Online content uses filters, editing, lighting and heavy make-up to make people look like they do. What do you think about this image? Do you think this is how this person looks in real life or has it been edited? How does looking at this image make you feel?

The bodies you see online are often of people who are not disabled. Why do you think that is? When you see someone with a visible disability on a video or TV, how does that make you feel?

As an adult you know that things can be faked online, but children take things at face value. As technology continues to advance with artificial intelligence (AI) and so-called 'deep fakes', recognising what's real and what's not is getting harder, even for adults. It's important to talk to children about the images they see online and help them develop critical thinking around them to avoid them being deceived by filtered and curated identities of online perfection. Real life is messy and imperfect, and seeing real faces and bodies with spots, scars and imperfections is important to help children grow to accept the body they live in.

The bullying conversation

Bullying is the act of repeatedly hurting another person, with words or physical actions, to cause them harm or humiliation, or in any other way to dehumanise them. It can include name calling, physically hitting or pushing, making threats and excluding a child from friendships or activities, and it is more likely to happen online if it already happens offline. Lots of children hide the fact that they're being bullied because they feel scared of retaliation from the bullies, so as a parent it's important you know the signs to look out for, including:

- Refusing to go to school
- Being anxious and tearful more of the time
- Becoming withdrawn and losing interest in things they used to enjoy
- Changes in their sleep patterns or appetite, such as struggling to sleep or snacking more
- Having unexplained bruises on the body or reporting that they fell (a lot!)

- Changes in their appearance
- A dip in their grades at school

If you notice these or other similar signs and think that your child might be getting bullied, you can take steps to safeguard their well-being.

- **Reassure your child it's not their fault.** When children are bullied, they start to believe that something's wrong with them. Reassure your child that there's no excuse for making others feel bad, and that it's the child or children who are doing the bullying who need to change their behaviour.
- **Brainstorm solutions.** Ask your child what they think might help them feel safe in places where the bullying takes place. If it's happening online, consider shutting down apps or sites where the bullying occurs while you create more safety for your child in the real world.
- **Advocate for your child.** Children often don't want teachers to know about bullying because they are scared of being a snitch. It's important that you speak up on behalf of your child. All state schools have bullying policies that include measures to prevent it. These policies are legally binding, and schools have a duty of care towards pupils during schooltime, as well as outside the premises if the perpetrators and targets of bullying both attend the same school.

Websites that can support you further

As parents we must stay aware of the online culture of today and provide our children with the information they need to lead full lives – both offline and online. These topics are relevant even when you choose to delay smartphones because your child may see, hear, or witness them on a different screen or device in or outside your home. Some useful websites that can help you carry on these conversations are:

- **NSPCC** (nspcc.org.uk): tips on online porn
- **Mental Health Foundation** (mentalhealth.org.uk): articles on bullying and body image in childhood
- **Internet Matters** (internetmatters.org): has a useful downloadable guide promoting positive body image
- **Kidscape** (kidscape.org.uk): bullying-prevention charity with information and guides for parents and young people, including those who are autistic
- **Young Minds** (youngminds.org.uk): information on all the above topics and more, with useful guides and information for parents

As you embed your Family Phone Pledge into your own and your family's lives, be mindful of how you use your smartphone, be intentional when you do so and focus on finding your SPARK: **Socialise** more face to face, take steps to be more **Present** every day in the real world, learn to **Access** the online world safely, prioritise **Rest** and sleep hygiene, and build your **Knowledge** on topics that can help you openly communicate and support your child online and offline too.

Remember, the best way to teach your child good digital habits is to model good technology use yourself. When you find your SPARK and embed strategies that stop you from getting lost in a screen, your child will learn how to do so too. Start small, be patient and keep going. Finally, if there are ever any times when you feel unmotivated or despondent, connect with your pledge parenting community and get a little boost to keep yourself on track. I'm rooting for you!

Step 7
Digital resilience

Children are growing up digital, but they don't have the protection they need to navigate the online world safely nor the digital skills to make the most of the opportunities it can bring. A report in 2023 called for a 'digital vaccination' for all children in the UK to ensure they have a minimum standard of digital skills. It detailed how half of all young people are teaching themselves digital skills and that three-quarters of those applying for jobs in 2030 will lack the basic digital skills needed to enter the workforce.

I found the data in this report surprising given what we know about smartphone ownership, but it's not shocking. Owning a digital device or having access to one doesn't necessarily mean you have the skills to use it appropriately or effectively. These must be learnt. Children and adults are engaging with online content without the appropriate skills, and given that digital literacy is crucial to children's futures, it's about time we focused on this in our homes, in educational provision and as a society.

My views on delaying smartphones are firm, but I don't believe in blanket restrictions on children accessing the internet. A UNICEF report studying eleven countries showed that children need to access the internet to build skills and resilience, such as problem-solving, critical thinking, and learning how to handle adversity and setbacks. Accessing the internet gives children opportunities to strengthen their ability to overcome obstacles in the digital world and in real-life situations too.[1] But access must come with safety. We need to safeguard our children in using the internet just like we teach them to cross the road. We first of all pick them up and carry them safely to the other side, and as they get older, we hold their hand and teach them to stop, look both ways and wait until the cars have passed. We apply safeguards, take steps with them, and teach skills with practice and repetition, until one day they're responsible and old enough to cross the road independently.

When it comes to the online world, we can do the same thing by choosing to take it SLOW.[2] This will make children safer and support them when building skills. Then, when the time comes for them to get a smartphone, they'll be equipped with the skills to handle it:

- Safety first
- Life skills
- Open dialogue
- Watch together

I know most of you will have already introduced some form of screen to your children, and that's OK. It's not too late to add in some of the steps I'm sharing with you to teach your children skills to be safe and responsible online, and if you've got this far there's little doubt that you're a thoughtful parent. Teaching our children digital skills doesn't have to be scary or complicated – we can truly go SLOW and make it easy for them, and for ourselves too.

Safety first

Safety is about allowing children to participate in age-appropriate online activities in age-appropriate ways while under active supervision. It's about encouraging them to extend their online experience beyond passive entertainment. And yes, this will inevitably expose our children to some online risks, but it's no different to what happens in real life. Our children are exposed to risk every time they cross the road or get into a car to go somewhere. All real-life activities carry risk, but we reduce them as much as we can by doing two things: taking responsible steps and safety measures, such as wearing a seatbelt and driving safely, and being available to support them when they need us.

Parental controls don't relieve you from parenting

Parental controls are not tools that teach our children about safe searching, privacy protection or media literacy. They're tools for us, their parents, to set up an additional layer of protection, but this is only appropriate in conjunction with you being there. No app, control or software can replace teaching children what to do when they see something that's scary or worrisome online.

Children can work around parental controls if they want to. They can adjust the clock to increase screen-time limits, use Google Docs as a chatting platform or find a backdoor to TikTok through Pinterest (yes, this is a real thing that children do. Just google it and find out!). In exactly the same way that we used to program the VCR to record shows for our parents, children can navigate parental controls much better than we can. Yes, we're the older generation now . . .

Parental controls take a lot of setting up and maintenance. They're often cumbersome, complicated and confusing, and rather than holding the tech companies who designed them accountable, they put the burden of monitoring onto parents. If you rely heavily on parental controls, you're going to be spending a lot of time monitoring your child's screen time on your own screens. It's a vicious cycle!

Parental controls are effective while your child is very young, but they're never going to be a viable long-term solution. If you want your child to be safe online there's simply no shortcut – you need to take an active stance in supervising them.

Life skills

Teach media literacy

Children's online and offline lives are often intertwined because they use the internet for education, creativity and socialising. At present, schools do not include media literacy as part of the curriculum, but supporting children in developing these skills is just as important as teaching them maths, biology or English literature. Children will grow up to be adults who use technology every day, just as we do. If we're going to help them to do so safely and tackle the spread of mis- and disinformation in a way many adults still don't know how to do, we should be making their media literacy skills one of our top priorities.

Safe online content resources

It is a minefield to make sense of what is and isn't appropriate online content for children, and the following resources will provide you with a great deal of useful information about online safety.

- *Parental control guides – internetmatters.org*
  Step-by-step guides for different devices and platforms to help you offer your child safe online experiences. From setting up your devices safely to choosing age-appropriate apps, tackling online issues and tips for online safety, this website contains a wealth of information. It's worth assigning some time to read through and familiarise yourself with all the information it provides. They also offer tailored support.
- *Ratings and reviews you can trust – commonsensemedia.org*
  An excellent website I refer to time and time again that gives age ratings and reviews for apps, films, games, podcasts and TV shows. They break down criteria by age, topic and genre so you can make informed decisions before downloading or visiting sites, and discuss this with your child too.

- **The Family Online Safety Institute – fosi.org**

  A toolkit made of short videos that walk you through how to navigate the internet with your children. This is an American site, so some of the language might not align with you as a parent, but I think it's a good first step towards thinking about digital safety with your children. The videos are short, which make them easy to listen to, think and discuss, and it's a good site to visit with a partner or as a group of parents during a pledge get-together.

- **Ofcom – ofcom.org.uk**

  The regulator for online safety in the UK. It protects you and your children from illegal content and activity online, including harmful content children may find or view. It is worth familiarising yourself with this website and what the online rules are, including for user-to-user content (such as social media), search services, video-sharing platforms, and where nudity and pornographic content might be visible. Ofcom is also the place where you can report concerns about anything you see online.

Media literacy is an educational framework that enables us be critical consumers of the online media we're exposed to.[3] Its core concepts are that all media messages are 'constructed' in one way or another, people don't experience the same media message in the same way (a child will respond to a meme completely differently to an adult), and most media messages are disseminated to gain profit or power.

To support you in teaching your child media literacy, here are five questions you can ask your child whenever they go online, be it for a school project, to send friends a message on the family laptop or when they become smartphone-ready.

1. **Who created this message?** What is its source? Can you trust it? What information helps you make this judgement?
2. **What creative techniques are being used to attract my attention?** How are they sharing this message in a way that makes you want to believe it?
3. **How might different people understand this message differently?** Would someone of a different age/gender/race/cultural background understand this message in the same way, or would they respond to it differently?
4. **What values, lifestyles and points of view are represented in – or absent from – this message?** Is the message inclusive or not? Who does it speak to most loudly?
5. **Why is this message being shared online?** Why did someone put it there in the first place?

Developing critical thinking is an important skill, and building this into children's online experiences is crucial to keep them safe. These five questions can assist your children in developing the intellectual tools that will help them to navigate and interpret online information more effectively. Write them on a Post-it note and keep it on your screen to review and reflect on, when it's appropriate to do so. Keep engaging your children in these conversations and build up a reservoir of healthy scepticism towards online information.

Teach your child to recognise 'red-flag' feelings

Red-flag feelings are the ones that make you feel uncomfortable, worried, sad or anxious. Depending on your child's temperament, they might clearly articulate their emotions, but others may find it harder to admit having uncomfortable feelings, naming them, managing them or even trusting that they're there at all. This is why it's necessary to teach children all about the mind–body connection and offer them tools to cope in these red-flag situations. When your children have clear steps they can follow, they'll be better able to make informed decisions.

The mind–body connection is the idea that how you think and feel is inextricably linked to how your body feels and functions. For example, if you feel worried, you might get a headache or stomach ache, your body might be more tense or feel tired or wired. On the other hand, when you're enjoying an activity and feeling safe, your body might be more relaxed and you might feel lighter. When it comes to engaging in online worlds, children can struggle to perceive physical feelings because their body signals in this context are muted, so asking children to notice what their body is experiencing and putting this into words is a huge task! Instead, I suggest you support your child in reflecting on their online experiences by focusing on four areas:

1. **How they feel.** Are they feeling sad, anxious, jealous, excluded or uncomfortable? Say to your child, 'If someone makes you watch something and you feel weird, scared, sad or disgusted, trust that feeling.'

2. **Identify what happened.** Was it something your child or someone else said or did? Try saying, 'No matter what happened, what you saw or what you did, you won't be in trouble. We'll believe you and do our best to help you. Things can be weird online, and we want to make sure you're safe.'

3. **What choices can your child make?** Are they able to make choices or do they need support? When thinking about this, consider their age and stage of development. This might sound like teaching your child to use assertive words like, 'I don't want to watch/do this' or 'This is scary, I don't like it,' and to seek help from a trusted adult. As your child gets older, their language might become more nuanced: 'This is unkind. I don't want to be involved' or 'I don't consent to you posting that photo/video,' while still knowing they can seek support from trusted adults at any time.

4. **Take active steps.** You must support your child to carry out these steps. Use role play and open conversations about these topics whenever you can, so when playdates happen, your past conversations reinforce the information and act as a reminder.

It can be useful to prepare your child before they spend time with friends who have smartphones and to ask them a few questions. For example, you might say, 'If a smartphone is around and you see something that makes you feel funny in your tummy, what can you do?'

Teach your child to say, 'I don't like it. I don't want to watch,' and remind them that they can get help from an adult or tell you about it when they get home. Give them a final reminder: 'You know you won't be in trouble no matter what it is, right? Love you! Have a great time!'

Modelling the mind–body connection that helps your child trust their 'gut feelings' is one of the most powerful methods of teaching, but it might not come naturally to you. The best way to become comfortable with it is to practise these steps yourself and role-model them to your child when the opportunity shows up. You could say something like, 'I feel a little shaken about something I saw online earlier today. It was a photo that made me feel uncomfortable. I decided I didn't want to see the photos or videos this person shares online any more, so I stopped following them and logged off. I had a warm drink and it made me feel much better.'

When you teach your child that being safe online is about being aware of the emotional impact it can have on them, they begin to learn skills that will support them in listening to the signals their bodies give them. These will offer them the intrinsic knowledge and motivation to stay safe online, even when you're no longer there beside them.

Open dialogue

Alongside keeping children safe when they explore, enjoy and learn about the online world, we must also build a relationship of trust. Even if you've signed up to the pledge with friends, there remains a possibility that someone around you will have a smartphone that your child will see, use or get access to. Rather than believe in complete abstinence, the thing that will keep your child safest is having regular open communication with you. The following are some things that are always worth doing with your children, but particularly when children go online or have access to their own smartphone.

Get curious about your child's online world

Being engaged in the things your child does online is no different to asking them about the things they did at school, who they played with, or what they enjoyed or found tricky. Try to become used to asking your child the same types of questions about their online worlds and 'digital playgrounds' too. If this is new or not something you've ever thought about doing, here are a few conversation starters to help you:

- 'What do you enjoy the most about this game?'
- 'What's the trickiest thing you have done on this app?'
- 'Who also enjoys playing this game? Do you ever talk about it/help each other?'
- 'What was the most frustrating thing that happened online today?'
- 'How did you feel while you were online drawing/playing/ watching something?'
- 'You were online for X amount of time. How are you feeling now?'

These sorts of questions don't just offer you useful information, they reinforce the importance of the mind–body connection that you've been teaching them about. Helping them reflect on what's happening to them in relation to their mind, their feelings and their body when they go online builds self-awareness (e.g. 'You feel a bit sleepy? Maybe you spent too much time online. Sometimes you might need to take a few minutes' break from a screen before you go back on. This will help your body and brain feel OK. Maybe use a timer when you do this next time and see how it feels?').

None of us can protect our children from all risk, either online or offline. What we can do is build relationships of trust that enable them to reflect, explore and develop coping strategies for when things go wrong. When they go through this alongside our supportive guidance, their experiences are undertaken in safety, even when they're sometimes left feeling a little shaky.

Don't expect your child to be honest, so build trust instead

This is a tricky one for many parents because we want to teach our children to be honest and we want them to learn that lying is bad. The truth is, we all lie sometimes. It's part of being human. And if you want your child to be more honest with you, there's no easy route to this: you've got to let go of harsh punishments, threats and shame. When children fear that honesty is going to get them into trouble, they're less likely to tell the truth. Our children will disclose more – and do it more willingly – if they perceive us as loving and supportive when they make mistakes, do things we asked them not to do or even when they tell a lie. When we focus on punishment or harsh consequences, the opposite happens: children tend to learn how to lie better, they do it more frequently and they're more likely to take greater risks behind our backs.

When it's time for your child to be honest about something they've seen, done or joined in with online or on their smartphone, they'll come to you with the truth if you've built a relationship of trust. And when they do, I want you to understand that the process your child has been through is their way of saying: 'I did something bad. I'm sorry, please love me and help me.' This is why your best response in that moment is not 'Why did you lie to me?' but instead, 'Thank you for telling me. I love you. I'm here for you.'

And your best next steps might be:

- **Find your calm first.** Breathe, drink some cool water, tell your child you need a moment or want to talk about it a little later. Take your time. It's not an emergency – it's best for you to be in the right mindset for this conversation.
- **Have an open conversation with your child and get curious.** 'Tell me what happened. You're not in trouble. I really want to understand.'
- **Shine a spotlight on your child's honesty, not your hurt feelings about the lie.** You might say something like, 'Thank you for talking to me. I know it was hard for you and I want you to know you can tell me anything.'
- **Problem-solve together.** You might then say, 'I don't want this to happen again to you, so what do you think we need to do? Have you got any ideas?' Offer your ideas too if it feels appropriate. Do you need to talk to teachers/parents/ friends? Do you have to set a limit on when your child sees certain people or ensure that they only go to certain homes with you alongside them? If you're concerned about other

children too, who do you need to speak to and how can you thoughtfully let them know something they might not be aware of?

There are no apps, technologies or even threats or prohibitions that can keep your child safer than you yourself can when you build a secure, trusting and open relationship. They need to know you're on their team and that whatever happens, you'll support them to get through it.

Watch together

Delaying smartphones is one of the ways to mitigate the risks of the internet, and this may work well in early childhood. Your child will consume the content that you curate for them. But as they get older they'll begin to watch content outside of your home and enjoy less of your protection. This is why digital resilience is a life skill – one that will serve your children well before and, crucially, after they get a smartphone.

Other digital devices, such as computers and tablets, allow children to go online but their larger screens are easier to monitor, and importantly, they don't offer quick access to social media in a pocket-friendly size. The day your child carries a smartphone will be a transitional shift into a different kind of digital life, as they begin creating and communicating in a digital ecosystem of their own choosing. To offer your child age-appropriate experiences online as they grow in independence, consider spending more time together online. Having these experiences within the security of your family home is an important transition that can embed healthy habits for life, rather than letting them have a smartphone at seventeen or eighteen, just as they leave the safe haven of your home and get lost in its many apps and sites without your close guidance or support.

Communal spaces and shared family devices

Before getting a smartphone of their own, using shared family devices can teach children responsibility and the vital skills of patience and waiting their turn. This might be hard at first, but it can be a great skill to teach children how to plan, organise and prioritise what they're doing. If we assume there's only a single device shared between all of you (there may be more!), it makes it more important that you take good care of it – things like being careful not to spill drinks over it or drop it on the floor, not losing the stylus from the tablet, and being thoughtful of others' needs by checking the battery so that the next person can use it while it's charged. These are no mere minor tasks, they're important steps towards learning how to be responsible with expensive digital items, and, if your child struggles with any of these steps, they can also serve as a useful point of reference when they ask, 'Why aren't I ready for a smartphone yet?'

On account of their size and lack of portability, laptops and tablets are less likely to be used impulsively or checked across the day than smartphones. So, when your child is smartphone-ready, you'll need to monitor your child's online use a little more actively and closely. You need to ensure they access age-appropriate content, help them navigate the pop-ups, ads and any links that show up, as well as establishing clear time limits so they continue to learn the importance of an offline/online balance. Following your pledge can help you ensure your child is using their phone in communal spaces where you can hear, see and be available to support them. This makes everything a lot safer for your child, and your support can help build their confidence and independence too.

Go online together

Digital play has often been perceived negatively, but video games can enrich play for children and their families when done in the right way. I love playing video games, and we've slowly started to introduce 'family' digital play. A few times a month we play *Wii Sports* or *Mario Kart*, which helps our eldest practise frustration tolerance and emotional regulation (because losing upsets her deeply).

We also have a subscription to Apple Arcade on our family tablet. We pay to have no ads and no in-app purchases, so it offers a completely closed digital platform where we know exactly what our child is playing (currently she only has two interests: Crayola Adventures for art and creativity, and Tamagotchi, a platform for puzzle and discovery games). This gives us confidence that the digital experience she has on these apps is enriching her play and skills building, not stunting them.

This is different to open digital game platforms such as Roblox, where allowing access means you're committing to investing ongoing time to curate the experience and ensure its safety. When children have their own smartphone, your task is to know what they're doing, who they're playing with and whether it's appropriate. This is a lot more fluid and difficult to monitor, so I suggest you involve yourself by spending some time learning about online games with your child and joining them in some of their digital experiences.

Playing video games together is fun and can teach your child healthy attitudes to gaming and important real-world limits. For example, we set an alarm to ensure we don't play for longer than forty-five minutes, and we talk about how video games can quickly and easily make us lose track of time. On those occasions when our daughter requests to finish a step before she saves her game (e.g. park the car in Tamagotchi or finish a drawing), we allow for this flexibility. To ensure our time limits are being adhered to, we sit beside her and watch her complete her task, we talk about what she is doing, we praise her skills or drawing, or just the fact that she is showing us something she enjoys doing online, and then we support her in turning it off. This also reinforces the importance of play as something that's social and should feel safe at all times.

Giving your child a smartphone

If you have been going SLOW with technology and building digital skills along the way, you will have prepared your child well for owning their first smartphone. The day you feel they are smartphone-ready, you must continue to support them in building digital resilience skills and layering knowledge to assist them in making informed choices. For example, help them think about their digital footprint, what they choose to share, their choice of words online and the picture these paint of them as a person in the real world.

Make conversations about your online activity a family habit. Keep this light-hearted and do it in everyday contexts, such as travelling in the car or sitting round the dinner table. Rather than asking a prodding question like, 'What did you do on your smartphone today?', talk about themes or topics that you've heard of and have open conversations about them. For example, if you want to discuss whether your child has seen or experienced misogyny online, ask them, 'Have you heard of Andrew Tate? Who are the boys talking about these days?' If you've read about the risk of dermatological problems from products that influencers share online and you're concerned about your child using them, ask them, 'Do you follow skincare or make-up influencers? What kind of products do they talk about?', and tell them a bit about what you know too.

In many ways, these are not different conversations to the ones you probably already have with friends who own smartphones, they're just about introducing them to your parenting context and not being scared of speaking up on topics or themes your child might see online. The better you understand your child's digital world, the better you'll be able to guide them.

Your child will keep some things private from you, and that's OK. By the time they are smartphone-ready, you'll need to accept that they'll have experiences they want to keep to themselves, but all the work you've already put in to protect and prepare them will mean that even when mistakes happen, it's you they'll turn to for support.

Keep nurturing your child's self-awareness, encourage them to recognise how they feel while they're online and renegotiate your Family Pledge as needed. As your child keeps learning, you can start to release some of the online parental restrictions so they can experience more of the internet and social media. This can help your child experience online independence while in the safety of your home, continuing to embed healthy habits as agreed in your pledge.

Learning to use a smartphone in this way is a gift that ensures your child has the skills to navigate the online world with far more maturity and dexterity than we probably ever possessed when we first got ours.

Conclusion

The greatest challenge

Delaying smartphones is the easy bit. I know it feels hard to say 'no', to listen to your child's constant pleas for a smartphone and to answer impossibly hard 'why' questions, but the waiting is not the hard bit. It's what we do during this time and how we create a rich enough world that children want to live in and engage with that requires the real effort.

If delaying smartphones is going to work, we must take the time to create sufficiently interesting worlds for our children and ourselves, ones from which we all have little desire to be distracted. When we're surrounded by smartphones that offer us instant gratification and have the power to whisk us effortlessly away from moments that bring discomfort, how do we create experiences and real-world activities that are alluring enough to keep us present to each other? There must be something worthwhile waiting for us on the 'other side' of putting our phones down. I mean, what exactly have human beings been doing for the last 100,000 years?

There have probably already been occasions when you've enjoyed life without a phone, but you may not have taken the time to notice these when they happened. I invite you to pause and ask yourself three questions. When you have no – or least very little – interest in reaching for your phone:

1. What are you doing?
2. Who are you with?
3. Where is this most likely to happen?

Jot down your answers, mull them over and consider how you can create more of these sorts of opportunities. For me, it's times when I'm outdoors exercising or doing an activity such as cycling, running, walking the dog, taking my daughter to practise her skating, skiing, swimming or playing tennis, or times when I'm with my family or friends, having a meal out, shopping, on a day trip or holiday. I'm most likely to forget to use my phone when I'm not at home doing mundane chores, when my brain seems to ask for an instant hit of distraction (which is why not having my phone on my person works). It seems paradoxical to me that I carry a phone to be contactable, but it's when I'm outside my home that I'm more likely to use it less. Unless it rings, I won't reach for it. I guess I don't need a distraction in those moments when I'm out in the world, interacting, socialising, living life.

Perhaps when we engage in more of these moments, we'll model to our children that phones aren't a crutch. They can be a useful tool, but we don't need to rely on them for everything.

You can delay your child getting a smartphone for as long as possible, but one day they'll get one, and with it gain unfettered access to the internet. This shouldn't scare you; it should help you recognise that delaying smartphones is a small step in a much bigger activity, which I think should begin with the question: 'What do adults need to do to get off their smartphones, so children don't see this as normal behaviour?'

Throughout this book, I've talked about how your behaviour sets the tone for your child's life. Most children grow up believing they need a smartphone, that it's an incredibly special, important item that's going to change their life. They learn that from us: what we do and how we relate to our phones. Whenever we pick it up silently and create a rupture in real-world conversation or interaction, whenever we laugh, get upset or tense up in the company of our precious phones, we inadvertently sideline our children. They observe our emotional reactions and see that these 'magical boxes' are all-powerful.

Whether we like it or not, we are our children's greatest role models. Children watch what we do all day, every day. So when we spend most of our time staring at a screen rather than being out there in the real world with them, it sends them a message that getting access to this key in our pocket to unlock the door to the internet is something essential. And perhaps children have a fantasy that with a smartphone, they can get a little closer to us, that we'll see them better, more clearly, because we're already in there, aren't we? It's ironic that when children get smartphones, most parents say something like, 'They've disappeared into a screen. I never see them any more.' Yet how often as adults do we stop to think: 'How many years did *I* not see them because of my phone? How many times did *I* ask them to wait because what *I* was doing on a screen was more urgent than them?'

Writing this down stings me greatly, so if you're feeling it too, please know that I share this impossible discomfort with you. And yet, my greatest hope is that as the adults we are, we can be mature enough to move through the emotions that acknowledging this reality provokes in us and find the necessary courage to take positive steps. In a world full of tech, our children may do best when they're the ones who can hold face-to-face conversations and speak confidently in person, have the skills to be engaging without filters or effects, demonstrate good critical thinking, and display human qualities such as kindness and empathy. These skills are best built offline and in their relationships with you. Taking the time to develop these skills is not time wasted, it's the key to the real world.

Never question the fact that your child prefers to spend time with you rather than with a screen. My entire professional career has been spent with children, and their *raison d'être* is to be seen, heard and loved by you. Children are desperate for our presence, even when their behaviour might trick you into believing otherwise. When they grunt at your questions about their school day or roll their eyes when you ask about their friendships, they're not rejecting you. You're simply asking the wrong questions or they're giving you a clue about their emotional map at that particular moment.

Stay patient, shift your language, be honest about how you feel and don't stop giving them real-world attention. Saying, 'Hey, I think I'm annoying you with my questions, but I miss you and want to know what you're up to when we're apart' is more likely to open up real talk than saying, 'Ugh, you're such hard work' or saying nothing at all and no longer asking them questions. Be devoted to being in a relationship with your child.

You can delay smartphones for your child and learn new habits with your own phone usage. This can work in parallel with your child. As they build patience during these waiting years, you can learn what waiting to use your phone looks like every day. And if you find this extremely hard, think of the empathy and compassion you're building in relation to your child's experience of not wanting to wait any longer. This reframing can help you to persist and stay engaged with the goal of protecting your child and keeping them safe for as long as possible. It's not the act of delaying that does all the work – it's you living the experience of delaying using your own phone that has the greatest impact. The Family Phone Pledge can help you create a parental community of support to act as a reminder that you're not alone. We're in this together.

And we need to remain realistic that just as we enjoy watching TV programmes, series and films, our children are going to get enjoyment and entertainment from screens too. Screens can be used to help us relax and unwind, and done with intention, can offer our bodies and brains a moment of rest. You'll never be able to fill up your child's time with 'ready-made experiences', and nor should you try to. It can be overwhelming for children to have too many clubs, extra-curricular demands and activities. Children need time to switch off, relax and unwind, and they need a lot more than we do because their brains get overstimulated faster. Offering children time for unstructured play, reading books for enjoyment, and calm, quiet activities like drawing, listening to music or crafting, can be useful ways to help them unwind. A screen can do this too, when it's a safe, enjoyable, age-appropriate show or film offered within a specified time limit. I don't want you to fear screens or erase them completely from your life, because I don't believe that's necessarily useful. Moreover, watching films and TV is great fun and can also be a wonderful way to have a shared interest with others. So don't worry if this is something you offer and if your child enjoys it too.

It's time we take more responsibility about the relationship we've created with smartphones. We can't place all the responsibility for building better habits on our children without modelling it to them in the first place. We can't tell our children to spend more time participating in real-life activities when we're not willing to be more present and do this with them. We've got to work at delaying our immediate need to be immersed in our online worlds alongside delaying access to them for our children. And we must create a richer, more interesting and engaging life as a society. We owe it to our children, and we owe it to ourselves too. And, of course, it's not all down to you.

We can keep pushing for tech companies to create platforms that are safe from the potential risks of grooming, exploitation, or being lured into watching violent and distressing content, in the same way we've got safety standards for the machines, gadgets and implements we use in our homes or the healthy standards we enforce on the choice of foods we consume. We should all be protected by safety standards when we enter the digital world, although our children's first line of protection has to be – and will always be – us.

None of this is easy, but all of it is possible. I truly believe we have it in our power to disrupt the smartphone status quo for the benefit of all. I pledge my commitment to do this with you, in my home, with my daughters. We only have one life, and it's not our online presence people will remember. It's the way we made others feel in our presence that others, and especially our children, will never forget.

Acknowledgements

I wrote this book on a tight deadline at a time when I wasn't sure I had this book in me to write. 'Am I the best person to write this book?' is the question I asked myself over and over. And then I remembered what a kind friend had said to me, 'If not you, then who?'

Once I started to put words on paper, the words seemed to pour out of me and I realised that what I wrote in this book had been thought about, mulled over and digested for over a decade. Around ten years ago, I regaled my husband on a car trip home about why I didn't think children should have a smartphone (it was the longest hour and a half of his life). At the time, I started to see children walking into my clinic room in the paediatric hospital I worked at holding mobile phones. 'It's a hand-me-down,' they would say. Mostly it was used for playing simple games and this felt pretty innocent given that finding something fun to do while you are in hospital waiting for hours is often a challenge for families. But I always felt uneasy that these expensive and powerful 'mini computers' were being given to children as young as six years old without any thought about the portal to the internet they opened them up to. Fast-forward to 2019 and having my first child, and the idea that she would one day have a smartphone was not something I feared. I have always known it will happen one day . . . but not yet. Writing this book has cemented all my thoughts and feelings about smartphones, and it has grown my confidence to delay them and hold my children's upsetting feelings when they come. I hope reading this book has done the same for you.

Thank you for supporting my work and choosing this book and, by doing so, being part of this new era of conscious, authoritative parenting. I will never take your support for granted; it's thanks to you that this book became an idea that turned into a reality. Parenting in 2025 is not easy. There is a lot of noise about what is 'right vs wrong', which might help build awareness but it can also get in the way of making the right decisions for you and your family. I hope you will see there is a way through that doesn't have to involve fear. It can be logical, compassionate and quietly rebellious of the status quo.

I'm deeply grateful to the incredible publishing team who brought this book to life with such care and commitment. Jane, your belief in this project and your passion for its message fuelled my writing more than you know. Thank you for championing every word. To the wider editorial team, thank you for your sharp eyes, steady guidance and gentle honesty that helped shape these words into their best form. It's been a true privilege to work alongside you all.

This book would never have come to life without the unwavering support of my incredible team: Alice R, Daisy and Alice K. Thank you for cheerleading me on, championing my work, holding space for my ideas, no matter how big or small, and never finding any request or query too much. Francesca, your 'watchful eye' and generous presence (even when you don't have to be), means more than I can say. I often pinch myself that you are my team and that I get to work with such brilliant and creative minds. Working with you never feels like 'work'. Thank you for your trust, your vision and your heart.

Special thank you to Professor Pete Etchells, for always making time to exchange ideas and explore the ever-evolving world of technology with curiosity and depth. And to Emma H, for your honesty, warmth and grounded presence. In a space like social media, which can often feel isolating despite its constant noise, I'm deeply grateful that it led me to the two of you.

Nothing I do is possible without the love, care and commitment of my husband who holds our family together when I run off into a room to write for days on end. My life would not be the same without this man, and I wouldn't be able to do half of what I do without my husband's constant support and encouragement. Thank you for always saying 'yes' when I need you to hold the fort and for telling me 'you can do it' when doubt sets in. You are my rock, and my heart will forever be happy that we chose each other.

And my daughters: I wrote this book at a time when you were both far too small to understand my 'why', but I hope one day, if you read it, everything will make sense. In many ways, this book is a long love letter from me to you. A way to make a formal commitment to being present and teach you how to use technology well so you can blossom into adulthood feeling confident, secure and loved. I know I won't have got everything right, but I hope that what I do will leave you feeling safe, seen and loved at the end of every day. I am so proud to be your mama. *Te quiero mi amor* (x2).

And last but not least, I want to thank my friends, but in particular: The Bowls Club collective, The Girls Next Door, the G Fam, the Gilroys, Steph Z, Isaac, Melanie, Caroline and Rachael, with whom over the past two years I have had countless open, honest, dilemma-filled and thoughtful conversations about smartphones. It is thanks to our conversations that I started talking about smartphones more publicly and that the 'Parent Phone Pledge' (AKA: our parent pact) began. I love you all for the humans you are and the incredible role models your children have in you. We might all be doing something different with smartphones in our homes, but we are all united in friendship, respect and commitment to doing the best we can for our children. In a world where fear and division seem to abound, it's your friendship that gives me hope.

Notes

Part One: The Wake-Up Call

1. Buda, T. S., Khwaja, M., Garriga, R. and Matic, A. (2023). 'Two edges of the screen: Unpacking positive and negative associations between phone use in everyday contexts and subjective well-being', *PLoS One*, 8(4).

2. Carter, B. et al. (2024). 'A multi-school study in England, to assess problematic smartphone usage and anxiety and depression', *Acta Paediatrica*, 113(10), 2240–2248.

3. Przybylski, A. K. and Weinstein, N. (2017). 'A large-scale test of the Goldilocks Hypothesis: Quantifying the relations between digital-screen use and the mental well-being of adolescents', *Psychological Science*, 28(2), 204–215.

4. Francisquini, M. C. J. et al. (2024). 'Associations of screen time with symptoms of stress, anxiety, and depression in adolescents', *Revista Paulista de Pediatria*, 43.

5. Tara, M., Zhang, L. and Lee, J. (2023). 'Identifying factors influencing online learning outcomes for middle school students during the

COVID-19 pandemic', *Education and Information Technologies*, 28(1), 123–145.

1 Safe

1. National Institutes of Health (n.d.). *Adolescent Brain Cognitive Development (ABCD) Study*. U.S. Department of Health and Human Services. Retrieved 11 May 2025 from https://abcdstudy.org

2. Miller, J., Millks, K. L., Vuorre, M., Orben, A. and Pryzbylski, A. K. (2023). 'Impact of digital screen media activity on functional brain organisation in late childhood: Evidence from the ABCD study', *Cortex*, 169, 290–308

3. Ferster, C. B. and Skinner, B. F. (1957). *Schedules of Reinforcement*, Appleton-Century-Crofts.

4. Livingstone, S. (2011). 'Internet, children and youth', in M. Consalvo and C. Ess (eds), *The Handbook of Internet Studies*, Blackwell, 348–368.

5. Center for Countering Digital Hate (15 December 2022). *Deadly by Design: TikTok Pushes Harmful Content Promoting Eating Disorders and Self-Harm into Young Users' Feeds*. Retrieved 11 May 2025 from https://counterhate.com/research/deadly-by-design/

6. Sean Coughlan, 'Most children sleep with mobile phone beside bed', *BBC News*, 30 January 2022, https://www.bbc.co.uk/news/education-51296197

7. Orben, A. and Przybylski, A. K. (2019). 'The association between adolescent well-being and digital technology use', *Nature Human Behaviour*, 3(2), 173–82.

8. Ferguson, L. J. et al. (2021). '*Like* this meta-analysis: Screen media and mental health', *Professional Psychology: Research and Practice*, 52(5), 386–396.

9. Przybylski, A. K. and Bowes, L. (2017). 'Cyberbullying and adolescent well-being in England: A population-based cross-sectional study', *The Lancet Child and Adolescent Health*, 1(1), 19–26.

10. Bickham, D. S., Hunt, E., Bediou, B. and Rich, M. (2022). 'Adolescent media use: Attitudes, effects, and online experiences', Boston Children's Digital Wellness Lab.

11. Weymouth, B. B. and Buehler, C. (2016). 'Adolescent and parental contributions to parent–adolescent hostility across early adolescence', *Journal of Youth and Adolescence,* 45(4), 713–729.

2 Seen

1. Seltzer, L. J., Prososki, A. R., Ziegler, T. E. and Pollak, S. D. (2012). 'Instant messages vs. speech: Hormones and why we still need to hear each other', *Evolution and Human Behavior*, 33(1), 42–45.

2. Barreto, M. et al. (2021). 'Loneliness around the world: Age, gender, and cultural differences in loneliness', *Personality and Individual Difference*, 169(110066).

3. Loades, M. E. et al. (2020). 'Rapid systematic review: The impact of social isolation and loneliness on the mental health of children and adolescents in the context of COVID-19', *Journal of the American Academy of Child and Adolescent Psychiatry*, 59(11), 1218–1239.

4. Roberts, J. A. and David, M. E. (2016). 'My life has become a major distraction from my cell phone: Partner phubbing and relationship satisfaction among romantic partners', *Computers in Human Behavior*, 54, 134–141.

5. C. S. Mott Children's Hospital National Poll on Children's Health (n.d.). *About the Mott Poll*, University of Michigan. Retrieved 11 May 2025 from https://mottpoll.org/about

3 Soothed

1. UNICEF Innocenti – Global Office of Research and Foresight (2024). 'Responsible Innovation in Technology for Children: Digital technology, play and child well-being', *UNICEF Innocenti.*

2. Ochsner, K. N. and Gross, J. J. (2008). 'Cognitive emotion regulation: Insights from social cognitive and affective neuroscience', *Current Directions in Psychological Science, 17*(2), 153–158.

3. Scott, F. et al. (2024). 'Children's digital play and well-being', *Research Report*, University of Sheffield, available at https://drive.google.com /file/d/1N3y-3goEjHbtMlWzOCT7UEmzicS90dNg/view?usp =drive_link

4. Siraj-Blatchford, J. and Whitebread, D. (2003). *Supporting ICT in the Early Years*, Open University Press.

5. UNICEF Innocenti – Global Office of Research and Foresight (2024). 'Responsible Innovation in Technology for Children: Digital technology, play and child well-being'.

6. Rosen, M. (2016). *We're Going on a Bear Hunt*, Walker Books.

7. Delahoyde, M. K., Tyack, C., Kugarajah, S. and Joseph, D. (2024). 'Insomnia and other sleep disorders in adolescence', *British Medical Journal of Paediatrics*, 8(1), e001229.

8. Gooley, J. J. et al. (2011). 'Exposure to room light before bedtime suppresses melatonin onset and shortens melatonin duration in humans', *Journal of Clinical Endocrinology and Metabolism*, 96(3), 463–472.

9. Duraccio, K. M., Zaugg, K. K., Blackburn, R. C. and Jensen, C. D. (2021). 'Does iPhone Night Shift mitigate negative effects of smartphone use on sleep outcomes in emerging adults?', *Sleep Health*, 7(4), 478–484.

10. Carter, B., Rees, P., Hale, L., Bhattacharjee, D. and Paradkar, M. S. (2016). 'Association between portable screen-based media device access or use and sleep outcomes: A systematic review and meta-analysis', *JAMA Pediatrics*, 170(12), 1202–1208.

11. Mireku, M. O. et al. (2019). 'Night-time screen-based media device use and adolescents' sleep and health-related quality of life', *Environment International*, 124, 66–78.

12. Carskadon, M. A. (2011). 'Sleep in adolescents: The perfect storm', *Pediatric Clinics of North America, 58*(3), 637–47.

13. The Sleep Charity (2021). *Sleep Hygiene.* Retrieved 11 May 2025 from https://thesleepcharity.org.uk/information-support/adults /sleep-hygiene/

Part Two: The Family Phone Plan
Step 2 Understanding your child

1. American Academy of Pediatrics (2021). *Beyond Screen Time: A Parent's Guide to Media Use.* Retrieved 11 May 2025 from https:// publications.aap.org/patiented/article/doi/10.1542/peo_document099 /79942/Beyond-Screen-Time-A-Parent-s-Guide-to-Media-Use

2. Blackwell, P. L. (2004). 'The idea of temperament: Does it help parents understand their fussy babies?', *Zero to Three*, 24(4), 37–41.

3. Stachl, C. et al. (2017). 'Personality traits predict smartphone usage', *European Journal of Personality*, 31(6), 701–722.

Step 3 Open and honest dialogue

1. Heck, I. A., Shutts, K. and Kinzler, K. D. (2022). 'Children's thinking about group-based social hierarchies', *Trends in Cognitive Sciences*, 26(7), 593–606.

2. Blanton, H. and Burkley, M. (2008). 'Deviance regulation theory: Applications to adolescent social influence', in M. J. Prnstein and K. A. Dodge (eds), *Understanding Peer Influence in Children and Adolescents, vol. 3*, Guilford, 94–121.

Step 5 Involving others

1. Ongcoy, P. J. B. and Tagare, R. J. (2024). 'The role of social support in shaping students' goal achievement', *The International Journal of Learner Diversity and Identities*, 31(1), 950–958.
2. Goodyear, V. et al. (2025). 'School phone policies and their association with mental wellbeing, phone use, and social media use (SMART Schools): A cross-sectional observational study', *The Lancet Regional Health – Europe, 101211.*
3. Weinstein, N., Vuorre, M., Adams, M. and Nguyen, T. (2023). 'Balance between solitude and socializing: Everyday solitude time both benefits and harms well-being', *Scientific Reports, 13,* article 21160.
4. Perrin, A. (2015). *Social Media Usage: 2005–2015*, Pew Research Center.
5. Orben, A., Tomova, L. and Blakemore, S. J. (2020). 'The effects of social deprivation on adolescent development and mental health', *Lancet Child Adolescent Health*, 4(8), 634–640.
6. Goldstein, A. N. and Walker, M. P. (2014). 'The role of sleep in emotional brain function', *Annual Review of Clinical Psychology, 10,* 679–708.
7. Crosswell, A. D. et al. (2023). 'Deep rest: An integrative model of how contemplative practices combat stress and enhance the body's restorative capacity', *Psychological Review,* 131(1), 247–270.
8. Eccles, D. W. and Kazmier, L. (2019). 'The psychology of rest in athletes: An empirical study and initial model', *Psychology of Sport and Exercise, 44,* 1–12.

9. Khouja, C. et al. (2022). 'Consumption and effects of caffeinated energy drinks in young people: An overview of systematic reviews and secondary analysis of UK data to inform policy', *British Medical Journal*, 12(2), 1–11.

10. Children's Commissioner for England (2024). *Annual Report and Accounts 2023–2024*.

11. Deiros Collado, M. (2024). *How to Be the Grown-Up: Why Good Parenting Starts with You*. Bantam Press.

12. Delfabbro, P. H., Winefield, A. H., Anderson, S., Hammarstrom, A. and Winefield, H. (2011). 'Body image and psychological well-being in adolescents: The relationship between gender and school type', *Journal of Genetic Psychology*, 172(1), 67–83.

Step 7 Digital resilience

1. UNICEF Innocenti (2025). *Prospects for Children in 2025: Building Resilient Systems for Children's Futures*, UNICEF Innocenti.

2. Power of 0. First Device Family Toolkit. Available from: https://powerof0.org/wp-content/uploads/2024/01/First-Device-Family-Toolkit.pdf

3. Share, J., Jolls, T. and Thoman, E. (2010). *Five Key Questions That Can Change the World: Lesson Plans for Media Literacy*, Center for Media Literacy.

Bibliography

Aronson, L. (2011). 'Twelve tips for teaching reflection at all levels of medical education', Medical Teacher, 33(3), 200–205

Barreto, M., Victor, C., Hammond, C., Eccles, A., Richins, M. T. and Qualter, P. (2021). 'Loneliness around the world: Age, gender, and cultural differences in loneliness', *Personality and Individual Difference*, 169(110066)

Bennett-Levy, J., Thwaites, R., Chaddock, A. and Davis, M. (2009). 'Reflective practice in cognitive behavioural therapy: The engine of lifelong learning', in J. Stedmon and R. Dallos (eds), *Reflective Practice in Psychotherapy and Counselling*, Open University Press, 115–135

Berger, M. N., Taba, M., Marino, J. L., Lim, M. S. C. and Skinner, S. R. (2022). 'Social media use and health and well-being of lesbian, gay, bisexual, transgender, and queer youth', *Systematic Review Journal of Medical Internet Research*, 24(9), e38449

Bickham, D. S., Hunt, E., Bediou, B. and Rich, M. (2022). 'Adolescent media use: Attitudes, effects, and online experiences', Boston Children's Digital Wellness Lab

Blackwell, P. L. (2004). 'The idea of temperament: Does it help parents understand their fussy babies?', *Zero to Three*, 24(4), 37–41

Bibliography

Blanton, H. and Burkley, M. (2008). 'Deviance regulation theory: Applications to adolescent social influence', in M. J. Prnstein and K. A. Dodge (eds), *Understanding Peer Influence in Children and Adolescents*, vol. 3, Guilford, 94–121

Blume, C., Cajochen, C., Schöllhorn, I. et al. (2024). 'Effects of calibrated blue–yellow changes in light on the human circadian clock', *Nature Human Behavior*, 8, 590–605

Buda, T. S., Khwaja, M., Garriga, R. and Matic, A. (2023) 'Two edges of the screen: Unpacking positive and negative associations between phone use in everyday contexts and subjective well-being', *PLoS One*, 8(4)

Carskadon, M. A. (2011). 'Sleep in adolescents: The perfect storm', *Pediatric Clinics of North America*, 58, 637–47

Carter, B., Payne, M., Rees, P., Sohn, S. Y., Brown, J. and Kalk, N. J. (2024). 'A multi-school study in England, to assess problematic smartphone usage and anxiety and depression', *Acta Paediatrica*, 113, 2240–48

Carter, B., Rees, P., Hale, L., Bhattacharjee, D. and Paradkar, M. S. (2016). 'Association between portable screen-based media device access or use and sleep outcomes: A systematic review and meta-analysis', *JAMA Pediatrics*, 170(12), 1202–08

Crosswell, A. D., Mayer, S. E., Whitehurst, L. N., Picard, M., Zebarjadian, S. and Epel, E. S. (2023). 'Deep rest: An integrative model of how contemplative practices combat stress and enhance the body's restorative capacity', *Psychological Review*, 131(1), 247–270

Delahoyde, M. K., Tyack, C., Kugarajah, S. and Joseph, D. (2024). 'Insomnia and other sleep disorders in adolescence', *British Medical Journal of Paediatrics*, 8(1), e001229

Delfabbro, P. H., Winefield, A. H., Anderson, S., Hammarstrom, A. and Winefield, H. (2011). 'Body image and psychological well-being in adolescents: The relationship between gender and school type', *Journal of Genetic Psychology*, 172(1), 67–83

Fibla, L. et al. (2023). 'Language exposure and brain myelination in early development', *Journal of Neuroscience*, 43(23), 4279–90

Fisher, P., Chew, K. and Leow, Y. J. (2015). 'Clinical psychologists' use of reflection and reflective practice within clinical work', *Reflective Practice*, 16(6), 731–43

Fletcher A. C., Nickerson P. and Wright, K. L. (2003). 'Structured leisure activities in middle childhood: Links to well-being', *Journal of Community Psychology*, 31(6), 641–59

Francisquini, M. C. J. et al. (2024). 'Associations of screen time with symptoms of stress, anxiety, and depression in adolescents', *Revista Paulista de Pediatria*, 43

Gooley, J. J. et al. (2011). 'Exposure to room light before bedtime suppresses melatonin onset and shortens melatonin duration in humans', *The Journal of Clinical Endocrinology and Metabolism*, 96(3), 463–72

Heck, I. A., Shutts, K. and Kinzler, K. D. (2022). 'Children's thinking about group-based social hierarchies', *Trends in Cognitive Sciences*, 26(7), 593–606

James, R. and Meredith, D. (2016). 'My life has become a major distraction from my cell phone: Partner phubbing and relationship satisfaction among romantic partners', *Computers in Human Behavior*, 54, 134–41

Junco, R. (2012). 'The relationship between frequency of Facebook use, participation in Facebook activities, and student engagement', *Computers and Education*, 58(1), 162–71

Katherine, V., Rusu, C., Quiñones, D. and Jamet, E. (2019). 'The impact of technology on people with Autism Spectrum Disorder: A systematic literature review', *Sensors*, 19(20), 4485

Khouja, C. et al. (2022). 'Consumption and effects of caffeinated energy drinks in young people: An overview of systematic reviews and secondary analysis of UK data to inform policy', *British Medical Journal*, 12(2), 1–11

Kushlev, K., Proulx, J. and Dunn, E. W. (2016). '"Silence your phones": Smartphone notifications increase inattention and hyperactivity symptoms', in Proceedings of the 2016 CHI Conference on Human Factors in Computing Systems, 1011–20

Livingstone, S. (2011). 'Internet, children and youth', in M. Consalvo and C. Ess (eds), *The Handbook of Internet Studies*, Blackwell, 348–68

Loades, M. E. et al. (2020). 'Rapid systematic review: The impact of social isolation and loneliness on the mental health of children and adolescents in the context of COVID-19, *Journal of the American Academy of Child and Adolescent Psychiatry*, 59(11), 1218–39

Miller, J., Mills, K. L., Vuorre, M., Orben, A. and Pryzbylski, A. K. (2023). 'Impact of digital screen media activity on functional brain organi zation in late childhood: Evidence from the ABCD study', *Cortex*, 169, 290–308

Mireku, M. O. et al. (2019). 'Night-time screen-based media device use and adolescents' sleep and health-related quality of life', *Environment International*, 124, 66–78

Odgers, C. (2024). 'The great rewiring: Is social media really behind an epidemic of teenage mental illness?', *Nature*, 628, 29–30

Operto, F. F. et al. (2023). 'Digital devices use and fine motor skills in children between 3–6 years', *Children (Basel)*, 10(6), 960

Orben, A. (2020). 'Teenagers, screens and social media: A narrative review of reviews and key studies', *Social Psychiatry and Psychiatric Epidemiology*, 55(4), 407–14

Orben, A., Tomova, L. and Blakemore, S. J. (2020). 'The effects of social deprivation on adolescent development and mental health', *Lancet Child and Adolescent Health*, 4(8), 634–40

Palmer, S. (2015). *Toxic Childhood: How the Modern World is Damaging Our Children and What We Can Do About It*, Orion

Przybylski, A. K. and Weinstein, N. (2017). 'A large-scale test of the Goldilocks Hypothesis: Quantifying the relations between digital-screen use and the mental well-being of adolescents', *Psychological Science*, 28(2), 204–15

Rosen, M. (2016). *We're Going on a Bear Hunt*, Walker Books

Scott, F. et al. (2024). 'Children's digital play and well-being', *Research Report*, University of Sheffield, available at https://drive.google.com/file/d/1N3y-3goEjHbtMlWzOCT7UEmzicS90dNg/view?usp=drive_link

Seltzer, L. J., Prososki, A. R., Ziegler, T. E. and Pollak, S. D. (2012). 'Instant messages vs. speech: hormones and why we still need to hear each other', *Evolution and Human Behavior*, 33(1), 42–5

Share, J., Jolls, T. and Thoman, E. (2010). *Five Key Questions That Can Change the World: Lesson Plans for Media Literacy*, Center for Media Literacy

Siva N. (2020). 'Loneliness in children and young people in the UK', *Lancet Child and Adolescent Health*, 4(8), 567–68

Stachl, C. et al. (2017). 'Personality traits predict smartphone usage', *European Journal of Personality*, 31(6), 701–22

Stiglic, N. and Viner, R. M. (2019). 'The effects of screentime on the health and wellbeing of children and adolescents: A systematic review of reviews', *BMJ Open*, 9(1)

Sun, J. and Miller, C. H. (2023). 'Insecure attachment styles and phubbing: The mediating role of problematic smartphone use', *Human Behavior and Emerging Technologies*, 2, 1–11

Tang, S., Werner-Seidler, A., Torok, M., Mackinnon, A. J. and Christensen, H. (2021). 'The relationship between screen time and mental health in young people: A systematic review of longitudinal studies', *Clinical Psychology Review*, 86

UNICEF Innocenti – Global Office of Research and Foresight (2024). 'Responsible Innovation in Technology for Children: Digital technology, play and child well-being', UNICEF Innocenti

Van Schalkwyk, G. I. et al. (2017). 'Social media use, friendship quality, and the moderating role of anxiety in adolescents with Autism Spectrum Disorder', *Journal of Autism and Developmental Disorders*, 47(9), 2805–13

Walton, G. M. et al. (2023). 'Where and with whom does a brief social-belonging intervention promote progress in college?' *Science*, 380(6644), 499–505

Weymouth, B. B. and Buehler, C. (2016). 'Adolescent and parental contributions to parent–adolescent hostility across early adolescence', *Journal of Youth and Adolescence*, 45(4), 713–29

Wittkowski, A., Garrett, C., Calam, R. and Weisberg, D. (2017). 'Self-report measures of parental self-efficacy: A systematic review of the current literature', *Journal of Child and Family Studies*, 26(11), 2960–78

Woolgar, M., Humayun, S., Scott, S. and Dadds, M. R. (2023). 'I know what to do; I can do it; it will work: The Brief Parental Self Efficacy Scale (BPSES) for parenting interventions', *Child Psychiatry and Human Development*, 1–10

Index